Goose River Anthology, 2018

Edited by

Deborah J. Benner

Goose River Press
Waldoboro, Maine

Library of Congress Card Number: 2018911877

ISBN: 978-1-59713-199-5

First Printing, 2018

Cover photo by Kasey Benner

Published by
Goose River Press
3400 Friendship Road
Waldoboro ME 04572
e-mail: gooseriverpress@roadrunner.com
www.gooseriverpress.com

Authors Included

Authors Included

Authors Included

Dedicated to
Oliver "Ollie" Owen Benner

Special thanks to Sue Campagna for her
wonderful help in proofing the book.

Goose River Anthology, 2018

Janice Babcock
Wauwatosa, WI

Entrepreneurship: It's the Berries!

Did you ever want something but didn't have enough money to get it? Well, that was my story. I was in fifth grade. An adult family friend, Bernice, had traveled and brought several purses back from Mexico with the intention of selling them. Imagine, they came all the way from Mexico! The purses had some unusual native design. I loved them! I wanted one of those brown leather hand tooled purses. I didn't have enough savings to buy it myself. It cost too much for my parents to purchase it for me. How could I get that purse?

My parents had what they still called a Victory Garden. This idea dated from World War II when food rationing and food stamps were used. Now it was the 1950's, but we still had a backyard garden. As a child, I was involved in tending our garden. Besides the usual vegetables like green beans, peas and tomatoes, we also had special patches of raspberries and strawberries.

I really wanted that purse. Then I had an idea. I asked my parents, "If we have extra raspberries or strawberries, perhaps I could sell them?" They thought about my proposal, and both parents answered, "Yes."

Wow! This was the answer I wanted. I proceeded to make plans to sell the berries.

I collected empty pint berry containers made of balsa wood from my friends. No cost there.

My garden picking gear was already in use because I was picking those berries for my family. The gear included blue jeans with rubber bands to put around my ankles to keep mosquitoes out, heavy shoes and a long sleeved shirt to keep bugs and sun away.

Grandma Josephine had already given me a homemade bonnet that she made during her farming days. For the brim, she cut cardboard strips for support, then sewed the strips

Janice Babcock
Wauwatosa, WI

using purple gingham fabric from one of her old aprons. The fabric draped down the neck as a shield from the blazing sun. I'm sure my berry picking costume looked quite hilarious, but I was happy to wear it.

The raspberries or strawberries were only available for me to sell if they were in abundance. Of course, I ate many of the raspberries or strawberries while picking them. I also had them to eat at our family table.

I kept abreast of current berry prices. I regularly walked to the local A&P grocery store to see the cost per pint of their berries. That comprised my marketing research technique. I undercut the grocery store price by charging my customers five cents less per pint of berries.

The store price range was about 25¢ to 30¢ per pint. My selling technique was door-to-door in person within my area for both raspberries and strawberries. Neighbors knew me, which helped my sales. I was a petite girl with a pleasant personality and cheerful smile that aided.

My selling points were, my berries were freshly picked that morning, the containers were always heaping full and were cheaper than the store. In addition, the berries had a sweet smell and bright red color. Of prime importance, I only picked them when they were fully vine ripened. In contrast, the grocery store's berries had to be picked somewhat green to allow for shipping time.

Picking raspberries was more challenging than picking strawberries. Their stalks had piercing barbs that easily pricked my skin or ripped my shirt. The raspberries were planted quite close together, making picking the berries among the stalks difficult. That bed of berries was full of mosquitos. Hate'em! On the other hand, strawberries were easier to pick, even though I had to bend over because they grew close to the ground.

The raspberries were the more fragile of the two berries. They did not have a long shelf life. The strawberries were more hardy. The raspberries were highly prized and some-

Janice Babcock
Wauwatosa, WI

times less available. Both berries were tasty. Raspberries and strawberries were truly a summer treat to be eaten plain or as part of a tasty dessert.

Keeping customer service in mind, if a neighbor was making a special dessert that needed a lot of berries, she could place an order with me. I would accommodate that need, if my parents agreed not to keep any berries of that day's picking. Now I was negotiating and becoming a business woman.

Our family friend, Bernice, hoped to sell the five to six tooled leather purses that she bought in Mexico. However, she saw my excitement about wanting to buy one of those expensive purses. She secretly held one purse back to see if I could earn enough money to pay for it.

Unfortunately, I was short about a dollar and a half from the quoted twenty-three dollars price for that leather purse. But I had the nerve to negotiate a lower price. Bernice had observed how hard I pursued my goal. She said, "I was impressed with your creativity and drive." That observation sealed the deal. So, Bernice yielded to my offer of a lower buying price. Now I was a young business woman.

I was thrilled with the new supple leather purse. I used it for many years to come. Although I no longer have the purse, the memories still linger. It was a true entrepreneurial experience for me.

Later, Bernice and her husband moved to Phoenix, Arizona. Recently, I had a nice telephone conservation with her. She is now ninety-three years old. She confirmed my recollection about my determination to earn the money to buy her imported leather purse. We both cherished those memories.

Mary Jane Mason
Larchmont, NY

Up Behind the Soybean Field

Over the two lane, dusty, barely-paved road
past the corn and soy and tobacco, to the cattle fence.
Through the cattle fence, up the dusty dirt road
alongside the pines and the skinny-dipping pond.
Up on the rise in the scorching heat
to the uncut grass, the weeds, the cactus trash heap.
To find the grave, cheek by jowl with the ancient
          moss-covered monuments.
The half hidden soiled slabs covered with dead grass
They lie there, hidden, forgotten, untended, segregated
unannounced, with no sign or fence, no clue, no honor.
They are neglected, unknown but to family.
Fathers, mothers, daughters, sons, even veterans
Lie unnoticed, unheralded, forgotten
behind the soybean field.

Steve Troyanovich
Florence, NJ

a vocabulary of silence...
for Jiddu Krishnamurti

the word
became orphaned
spawned
from torn sorrows
in a motherless land

abandoned in fluttering isolation
the wingless pronouncements
of sodden empires
presumed to speak...

there were no
more words
no more worlds
to understand

***

while the stars wept...
Your love has taught me...how to be sad.
—Nizar Qabbani

you braid my dreams softly
within the playful existence of lingering moments...
your fragrance finds my sleep...
tasting forever is the promise of your lips...
tonight memory searched your face...
an autumn moon held your eyes...
loneliness wore the facade of your smile...

Carolyn Locke
Troy, ME

eclipse

your body curled like a fetus
you wait
beside the open window

hear only the faint
rustle of leaves
a dog barking in the distance

crossbeams of light
emanate from the moon
probing deep within you

and heart cells quicken
as earth's shadow creeps
across her bone-white face

just before total darkness
a slim golden crescent
rims her outer edge

then disappears and you feel
the moon pulsing ruby red
while all around her

glittering stars explode
drawing you back
to that celestial sea

original and infinite breath

Sylvia Little-Sweat
Wingate, NC

Sea Lions

Old males
asleep
on slimy rocks
in the sun scratch
themselves awake
lift
whiskered
heads
to roar
yellow-toothed
at the surf.
Celibate
they
must
wait
to mate
until the season
turns
like the tide.

Thomas Peter Bennett
Silver Spring, MD

Forest Sunrise

Foggy morning in the forest,
an owl hoots. A drop of dew
slides down a leaf's curve.
Dawn mist outlines
spider webs.

The color spectrum shifts
from violet to cerulean,
from rose gold to velvet blush.
Leaves are transfixed
in a crystal scene.

Sunrise is brightening,
with subtle silver pastels
and glistening treetops.

***

Peggy Trojan
Brule, WI

Tanka

I moved the peony
you and your house both gone now
it will bloom next year
ants crawling on the fat buds
the heavy heads drooping pink

Goose River Anthology, 2018//8

Juliana L'Heureux
Topsham ME

Bringing Lourdes Home

Lourdes is a town and shrine in southwestern France, in the foothills of the Pyrenees Mountains, near Spain. It's known for the Notre-Dame de Lourdes Sanctuary, a major Catholic pilgrimage site. Each year, millions visit the Grotto of Massabielle (Grotto of the Apparitions) where, in 1858, the Virgin Mary is said to have appeared to a local young woman. In the sanctuary's grotto, pilgrims can drink or bathe in water flowing from a spring.

Healings, cures and miracles have been attributed to those who have made religious pilgrimages to Lourdes. Most of the experiences are rooted in faith. There is evidence about how the human spirit and a desire to achieve a higher level of religious devotion are strengthened as a result of attending the religious renewals, as they are organized at the religious shrine.

Our personal journey to Lourdes created a curious result because it occurred after we returned home. We experienced an unexpected outcome related to an unusual conversation my husband had with a vendor in the French town's busy shopping district. Our story demonstrates how there are many ways of experiencing the miracles of Lourdes.

Yet, while at the Sanctuary and shrine, we spoke with several people who explained how they had been helped by visiting Lourdes. One middle-aged Irish lady who we spoke with was pushing herself in a wheelchair. She explained to us how there had been a time when she was unable to physically get herself out of bed.

With a beaming smile, she described how pushing her own wheelchair was the result of a physical healing she attributed to her several pilgrimages and devotions at the shrine. Another healing was described by my next door neighbor, back in Maine, who gave me a letter written by her

Juliana L'Heureux
Topsham ME

mother in response to our visit to Lourdes. Her letter described how she had experienced a short remission to her chronic autoimmune disease and she felt this had been a result of giving us her name to submit to the shrine's grotto, where the faithful pray.

Our personal story was more pragmatic, rooted in a practical experience, more than it was about a physical healing. We didn't realize the significance until we had returned home to Maine.

For those who might be unfamiliar with the Lourdes shrine, the history of the pilgrimages began with a series of apparitions of the Virgin Mary to a local peasant girl who lived in the town. Mary appeared to Bernadette Soubirios (1844–1879) on eighteen occasions. The first apparition was on February 11, 1858, and last one was on July 16, 1858. Several physicians examined Saint Bernadette to confirm her mental stability and it was eventually determined, by the Roman Catholic clergy, that her experiences were supernatural and divine.

During the past 150 years, since the mystical events occurred, the numbers of pilgrims who have visited the Lourdes shrine for spiritual and healing renewals have been reported to be six million people annually.

Lourdes consists of two distinctly different communities. One is the religious Sanctuary at Lourdes, the site where the apparitions occurred. On the other hand, the town of Lourdes is a busy community where local businesses focus on accommodating the millions of pilgrims.

In the town of Lourdes, the residents live alongside the bustling businesses, hotels and guest houses. While we were walking along the busy sidewalks with thousands of pedestrians, my husband felt like he was experiencing the aromas he was familiar with when his mother was cooking meals in their family's kitchen. I was unable to share his special olfactory sense but this experience followed him throughout our Sunday morning stroll, while walking from our hotel to

Juliana L'Heureux
Topsham ME

the Sanctuary, where we attended Mass. When we were inside the Sanctuary grounds on that Sunday morning, we followed a group of German pilgrims into one of the many chapels located on the property and we stayed with them for morning Mass.

But, back in the town of Lourdes, we obviously took advantage of some shopping. Our interest wasn't in purchasing the typical religious artifacts. We stayed away from items that were easily found in nearly all religious stores, regardless of where they happened to be located. Instead, we were looking for something special, although we weren't sure what that something might be.

Eventually, a particularly brilliant decoupage picture caught my husband's eye. It's a popular image of a young woman carrying a baby. In the composition, the young woman could be any mother because she's not a typically holy subject. The title of the picture is "Madonna of the Street," by Roberto Ferruzzi. In the image, the young woman is clothed in a blue cape and she wears a loosely fitting gold printed headscarf. In her arms she holds a sleeping baby who is dressed in a white gown. Some interpret her to be a homeless mother.

To our dismay, when we tried to purchase the picture, the shop keeper quoted an outrageous price, well beyond the amount we were willing to pay.

Consequently, my husband and the shop keeper engaged in an argument. Obviously, the shop keeper was surprised when he found himself arguing with an American who could speak French. One advantage to being able to speak French fluently is the ability to calculate numbers and discuss the prices and costs of commodities. In French, the numbers beyond fifty are translated as though they are Roman numerals. Therefore, the number 70 is "soixante-dix" or "sixty plus ten." Numbers in French become even more hyphenated when a customer and a seller are trying to barter on an agreed upon price. Unfortunately, it didn't take long before

Juliana L'Heureux
Topsham ME

the fluctuating prices and the numbers were flying back and forth between the two men, while the discussion became quite animated. In fact, the shop keeper finally escorted us out of his shop and closed the door, ending the negotiations. We did not purchase the picture.

Back home in Maine, I kept thinking about the picture when I was surprised to find another one, exactly like the Lourdes' image. This one was for sale in our parish's church gift shop. I was pleased when the price tag on the parish picture was not "soixante-dix" dollars. Instead, the price was nine dollars and, yes, it was exactly the same picture and one I could easily afford.

I purchased the affordable "Madonna of the Streets," the same one we saw in Lourdes, as a gift for my husband on Father's Day.

Yet, there was still more to end this Lourdes' story.

A few years later, after our Lourdes, visit, we decided to put our house up for sale. Lourdes came back home when the "Madonna of the Street" was a deciding factor to a family that was looking to purchase our house.

We were worried about finding a buyer because a contract to move into our brand new home was nearing a closing date. Therefore, we were anxious to sell as we prepared for the closing on another mortgage. When the realtor took the prospective buyers through our house for sale, the image of the "Madonna of the Street" hanging on a bedroom wall was perceived as a sign that our house was the right one for them to buy. We sold the home to the family because the wife and mother kept a photo card image of the very same picture in her wallet. Indeed, the family still lives there.

Our experiences in Lourdes were lovely in a spiritual sense and rather ordinary when it came to our interaction as tourists, trying to deal with an unreasonable shop keeper.

Indeed, there are many small and pragmatic ways to experience miracles from Lourdes.

We brought Lourdes home with us. In a spiritual sense,

Juliana L'Heureux
Topsham ME

the encounters we experienced remain in our hearts as being uplifting and affirming of our faith.

Yet, our pragmatic memory of bringing Lourdes home continues to adorn the bedroom wall in our house.

***

P. C. Moorehead
North Lake, WI

Wild Mountain

The wild mountain summons me.
I must go—the wild mountain calls.
I must trip and find my way.
I must go.

Wild lichens cannot hold me,
wild beasts not stop me.
The mountain calls.
I must go.

No water holds me.
No tree binds my path.
I am wild.
The mountain—I must go.

No trail too dark,
no path too steep—I go.
The mountain—
I must go.

Goose River Anthology, 2018//13

Robert B. Moreland
Pleasant Prairie, WI

Boston Harbor Light

Sentinel on Little Brewster Island,
tower bulwark for century and a half
stands the matron widow in the harbor,
light keeper long since gone.

From the seawall in Hull blessed breeze,
seagulls sing in melancholy cacophony.
Day draws to a close, summer's twilight,
sun waxing for the plunge westward.

How many years has she saved
storm-tossed sailors and bound safe
entry to the harbor between the islands
fresh painted white dress, picture perfect?

I, too sail the storm tossed seas of life
with canvas double-reefed, pumps stressed—
roll with huge breakers to dash my cargo,
strain to find the light to take me home.

The sun sinks down past the horizon,
colors rich begin to blossom and bloom.
Brilliant red sky at night, sailors delight,
Venus peeks through developing darkness.

Countless stars as many as Your love,
twilight fading, wink on but one at a time.
Dear Father, your love richly embraces me
and I know in my heart, it will be all right.

Miner, K.M. and Moreland, R.B. *Eternal not Immortal: Poems,
prayers and promises for the journey of life.* **Trafford Publishing**
(Victoria, B.C., Canada, July 2005), page 155.

Andrea Suarez-Hill
Jonesboro, ME

Sea Change

Fish-heavy boats
plow down the reach
reeking bait and diesel.
Black-backed gulls arc
high to dive at scraps.
Sun-coated seals snooze
on hump-back stone, and
ocean swells sprawl over
mammoth storm worn walls.

A 9.9 Mercury hums a mantra
from Amesbury transom and,
deft as green crabs, we hop over
splintered dock pilings, hitch our skiff
to raid a private island. We pirates
jump a faded "No Trespass" sign,
race a falling tide
over broken boardwalk
to an unmanned light.

Hand-wrought door hinges and
a handle keepers once touched open
on moss-covered brick and mortar.
A spiral rust-stained staircase
leads to Stone Age tech that
once flashed its own code in crystal
and sounded a horn
sailors sought and obeyed.
We high-five the view.

E.M. Barsalou
Kittery Point, ME

Breathe

In a lighter time when the sun shown bright,
Morning altered the days that faltered shadows
Existing on the side of the barn.
The old tree, in it a swing that hung by chains not by rope.
A splendid way to keep up your hope and pride.
An instant smile comes to mind
Playing as a child all the while lost in time.
In the back forests behind our home,
Out in the blueberry fields where I would roam,
Climbing the old rock wall, from below the acres like a
        fence to gate you in.
Alas, was not that at all, but a place of great adventures,
Expanse of mountains ranged around the lake.
The barrens of blue, it' s not hard to explain.
Withered with Indian dreams, in starlit northern skies
        indeed.
A pleasant way to learn about the day when life was quaint
And fully sufficed to express your mind.
It just gives way the drawings of dreams, playing in the
        hay.
Rustic overtones from the common locals heathed,
Working for the promises of a free land to just simply
        breathe.

Gina Montini Mosca
Augusta, ME

The Witness

It was late in the afternoon and we were bored. She was six and I was three. I had no idea what I looked like at the time or what I was wearing. I, of course, was more focused on her. Sissy was my big sister and I was concerned with every move she made. I looked up to her for direction and guidance. She had no idea how much I worshiped her or longed for her acceptance.

We had been cooped up all day because it had been raining. Earlier in the day we had climbed up on the couch to look out the front picture window. "See the ballerinas?" she said. I was filled with awe as I watched the raindrops pelt onto our front porch and the concrete sidewalk below. I knew exactly what she meant. The dropped rain spun around the same way the ballerina with the white taffeta skirt whirled to the music when I opened my little white jewelry box.

It was close to dinner time. Sissy begged our Mama to let us go outside to play. "It has stopped raining and the sun is shining, can we go out now?" she pleaded. "Not now," Mama replied. "Wait until Daddy comes home."

For the next hour, I chased Sissy around the inside of our house trying to keep up with her. She wore a pink short-sleeved cotton button down blouse. The sleeves were gathered at the end with elastic.

Her pants were green corduroy. She had short strawberry blond hair. A small amount of her hair was clumped together to form a tiny ponytail which looked like a fountain atop her head.

As Mama prepared dinner, I chased pink and green from room to room. The smell of pork chops frying on the stove was appealing to me as my belly recognized hunger. As hungry as I was, I starved more for Sissy's affection.

Gina Montini Mosca
Augusta, ME

I chased pink and green to the couch for the hundredth time. We stood against the couch and looked out the window. I saw my red tricycle and Sissy's pink big girl bike with training wheels on the front porch. The sun had started to dry the rain that had drenched our locomotives. People were walking outside again. As usual, the man in the tan trench coat walked by holding the arm of a woman whose head bowed down like she was admiring her red Ked sneakers.

Sissy pushed the gold burlap curtains wider to get a better view outside. I played with the large fabric covered buttons which were affixed at the center of our couch's puckered cushions. We waited anxiously for Daddy to arrive. We would greet him with squeals and hugs and then he would take us to the backyard to play while Mama continued to prepare the meal.

The house seemed still and I had no awareness of where my four older brothers were at the time. The peacefulness was peculiar. I wasn't worried about who would get to greet Daddy first. I was the sixth child, the baby of the family, and I was always last. I just wanted to be parallel with my sister and greet him by her side. Sissy hadn't wanted to be my equal. She was older, smarter, faster, and at times she seemed to be pleased with her conquests. I just wanted to be accepted by her. I wanted her to like me as much as I liked her but I always felt the weight of rejection.

The rush of excitement regarding Daddy's arrival intensified. As we stood on the couch looking out the front window, we extended our heads to the right to look down Hawthorne Avenue. We bounced up and down with anticipation. Finally, the moment arrived. From around the bend we spotted Daddy's Dad's tan Ford Falcon advancing up the road towards our house.

In a flash, Sissy leaped off the couch and made a U-turn to our front foyer. I, her faithful shadow, jumped off the couch and clumsily followed in her direction. The thick brown wooden inner door was already open but the storm

Gina Montini Mosca
Augusta, ME

door was closed. Sissy raced towards the storm door, smacked the handle with her right hand and pushed against the metal frame to open it wide enough to slip out. Like numerous times before, I followed several steps behind. I extended my right arm to stop the glass paneled door from closing. The spring forcefully contracted and at that instant life seemed to propel in slow motion. As the force of the closing glass door met my small, three year old body, the large plate of glass shattered. As I crashed through the metal frame, a large serrated blade of glass sliced my right arm from the length of my dainty wrist to my underarm pit. As blood spewed out of my body, I felt myself falling. My body felt heavy and I was paralyzed with fear.

Suddenly, a warm sensation engulfed my entire body. At that moment, I truly saw myself for the first time. I was floating up towards the foyer ceiling and I looked down and saw me- a little girl with golden locks lying on the front porch in a pool of blood. I was wearing a white short sleeved cotton shirt and light blue corduroy pants. In a flash, I saw Daddy park his car and race up the front sidewalk. He flipped my body over onto my back. Looking down, I saw my huge deep set blue eyes which appeared frozen and dazed. Daddy screamed at Mama directing her to get something to make a tourniquet. Our neighbors rushed onto the porch to help.

Mama stormed into the dining room and my eyes followed her. She clutched my new Dr. Denton pajamas which were set on top of the brown hutch. The P.J. bottoms were a solid pink and had white feet. The pajama top had pink sleeves and a white center. The shirt was adorned with balloons and the words "Happy Birthday" across the center. As Mama raced toward the porch with my bed clothing, I cried "No, not my new Happy Birthday pajamas" but no one seemed to hear me. Mama sobbed hysterically and continuously chanted "no no baby, hang on." She handed the pajamas to Daddy and then dropped by my side. Daddy lifted my limp body off the porch and placed me in my mother's lap.

Gina Montini Mosca
Augusta, ME

He tied the solid pink bottoms around my arm and instructed Mama to apply more pressure.

In a rage, Daddy yelled at Sissy and threatened her with a spanking when he returned. I looked down and saw Sissy kneeling on the steps weeping. Her tiny hands covered her eyes in attempt to deny the bloody reality displayed before her. Surprisingly, she now looked small and vulnerable to me. My heart ached for her; I longed to hug and comfort her.

Frantically, Daddy picked me up and he and Mama raced to the car. Daddy carefully placed me in Mama's lap. As the tan Ford Falcon raced to the hospital, Mama sobbed and Daddy accusingly screamed at her, "Why weren't you watching them, were you drinking?"

"No, I was cooking your dinner," she refuted defensively.

My little body was flaccid and Mama kept shaking me pleading, "Hold on baby, hold on baby, don't leave me." At that moment, I felt a huge sense of compassion for my parents. I saw how young and imperfect they were. I was no longer a three year old baby, I was a wise witness to all that was unfolding.

***

Patrick T. Randolph
Lincoln, NE

Dr. Taxi Driver

She asked for a ride
To the other side of town,
He knew she was ill—

Diagnosing everything—
Inside his rearview mirror.

Susan van Alsenoy
Wiscasset, ME

Quarting

Turn in at the horseshoe drive laid on a
Neatly-kept hill where a red farmhouse
Nestles between red and blueberry barrens.

In the barn behind are worn packing tables,
And the wooden winnowing machine,
Little changed, but no longer run by hand.

Bushels of fruit fresh from fields in—
Baskets of cleaned blueberries out.

Whirling floor fans keep purple berries,
And busy, bluing workers, cool and dry.
Waiting quart cups of cardboard laced with vents
Once filled, are topped with punched cellophane,
and sealed shut with rubber bands.

"Be sure to overfill the boxes—
Careful those corners—the berries will lose
Volume overnight as they respire."

Many friends, many hands, breathing and working
Side by side, make such chores like this
Ones of pure delight as day dims into night.

Paul G. Charbonneau
Rockport, ME

More than Meets the Eye

How come night is so dark,
the cosmos best seen dimmed?
A trillion plus galaxies
swell with countless stars
bewilderingly bright.

Distances fathomed
in years of streaking brilliance
barely let celestial light
get through to me,
then blind my mind's eye.

Is it not always dawn
when light source
after light source
sets fire
to every horizon?

While earthly sightings
change sunshine to darkness,
I grope about anyway,
led by the warmth
of a tiny flame

inherited at birth.

Sarah J. Woolf-Wade
New Harbor, ME

Good Old Men

I have known some good old men
the finest men in anyone's world—
no longer wild or temperamental
no pouting or pursuing cloud formations,
skirts, or changing tides.
Poets, philosophers, scientists, friends
patient and positive
no longer robust but stout of mind
remembering sweetness of yesterday:
Silent John with his pipe in his teeth
suffered students with straying thoughts;
Tom, gentle companion in shadow
at Robert Frost's northern farm;
Francis, blind, a head bursting with poems,
eager to hear the words from pages,
humble, grateful, kind;
Alden, recalling minutia of youth,
mountains, deserts, canyons and oceans
overflowing with achievements.
They all listen and endure,
do not lecture, judge, complain
of blindness, loss, disappointment, pain.
Hold on to today, let go of sorrow
and never, ever, mention tomorrow.

First published in *Wolf Moon Down* by **Goose River Press**.

Sally Belenardo
Branford, CT

A Very Purple Violet

Mornings such as this are few
that blossom forth from dawn
with birds in a nest on a lilac branch,
and jewels, prong-set in blades of grass,
aglimmer on the lawn,

where I find a deer mouse dead beneath
a very purple violet and a heart-shaped leaf.

Early sunlight covers
his wet fur and whiskered muzzle
with a sprinkling of crystals, as it were.
His half-open eye is bright, his tiny paws curled,
trying to grasp what stopped him
in his track, made him blind and deaf,
and took away his breath,

ending a span of two years or less,
and winter spent holed up in darkness
so he wouldn't freeze.

Adding a tear to the dew
or a sigh to the breeze
won't change that it's hardly reward for a wight
whose treasures were seeds,
and his life lean and brief,
to rest in raiment worthy of a king
on a morning such as this, beneath
a very purple violet and a heart-shaped leaf.

F. Anthony D'Alessandro
Celebration, FL

Scars of War

"Michelangelo Milano, loving husband...devoted father..."
My eyes scoured the newspaper obituary. I clutched that
offensive, twisted tabloid four different ways in four seconds.
Finally, I strangled it with my right hand and pressed it tight-
ly against my chest. Perhaps my sweaty and strong stabiliz-
ing hold would miraculously change the gut wrenching story
staring me down.

I tried to deflect that gloomy news by stretching toward
the awakening autumnal sun in preparing to unveil her glo-
rious wares on that crisp Montauk, Long Island morning. My
teeth chattering, Madame Moon blinked coyly as she slowly
vacated a drab gunmetal-sky. What, no celestial spectacu-
lars today? Then again, how would the moon and sun read
my feelings? Sunrise finally affirmed its auspicious debut. I
prayed that I'd been dreaming or misreading the news page.
Reality disregarded my wishes. The finality of human mortal-
ity jarred me. The cruel cold truth announced by that printed
page pummeled my defenseless soul. My friend Milano had
died.

Michelangelo Milano still seemed dashing and alive to
me. Despite my moist reverie, I saw him clearly. Mike, as I
called him, had been my closest friend for a short five-year
window. A gaunt, David Niven look alike of two score years,
his motor never appeared to flutter. He sported a sleek,
arrow-like straw colored mustache that looked penciled in.
We worked for a popular small-town newspaper and
assigned interviews within our tri-state area. Occasionally,
during our travels, Mike dozed off in the car. An internal
alarm awakened him as we approached the homes of the so-
called famed interviewees assigned us. My buddy often
seemed smarter and superior to the prominent people we vis-
ited. When incessant car chatter induced him to nod off, he

F. Anthony D'Alessandro
Celebration, FL

made demands between snores. "Put the easel
there! No, more shading! That's all wrong! Redo it!"

I never told Mike that his walk reminded me of a wounded leopard stalking its prey. Occasionally, my eye detected an almost imperceptible limp in his gait, perhaps caused by an errant shot from a crazed hunter on one of his frequent hunting treks. I recalled his limitless imagination. He heard arias when I heard songs. He crafted beauty out of what I tossed away in the garbage pail. He saw stairways to heaven while I complained of hellish and dreary storm clouds to Hades.

Multi-talented, Mike published poetry, designed billboards, cereal boxes, and packages that dominated store aisles. One of his unique seaside paintings hung from my den wall and except for its lack of ocean breezes and salty aromas, it furnished a realistic magnificent island life to that room. An artist, he proved stereotypically eccentric, brilliant, and opinionated. I frequently amused myself at breakfast when I examined his sketches pasted to my breakfast cereal box.

Mike kept his aeronautical degree a secret from me until he began inviting me to technical lectures about the history of flight. One arctic night, even before I could brush the slushy snow off my boots and sit with a group of smiling glad-handed guests at an aircraft lecture, he squeezed my right elbow and commanded, "Let's get out of here, Petey!"

"What are you talking about, we just got here?" I answered in a muzzled growl. I added, "Besides, I don't feel like going back out into Long Island's dime store version of Siberia. We've discovered a welcome shelter here. Let's stay and relax by this fireplace and relish its warming embrace, "I pleaded with raised arms.

He whispered in my ear, loud enough for those seated in front of us to turn around.

"They are all jerks in this place."

I suggested that he spend some time with his fellow club members.

F. Anthony D'Alessandro
Celebration, FL

"Why not hear them out? Give them a chance," I said.

After groaning and moaning he yanked my elbow from my seat like a boater would pull his stubborn rowboat to dock, "Come on, Petey. Just listen to them. Look at all those yawners. They're all jerks. I know jerks when I see them," he said. So we trudged out into an inhospitable frosty night where every breath I took appeared as noticeable as an elephant on a ballet stage.

Mike remained steeped in loyalties, especially regarding art, perfection, and honesty. He refused to tolerate anyone failing to meet his lofty standards. A few weeks later, I watched Milano win his election for the presidency of a local photography club, just one vote shy of unanimous. Sporting a wide smile, I said, "Pretty popular, eh?"

"Not popular enough. Some *cafone* (low life) voted against me. I'm quitting!"

"Quitting? You just won an overwhelming vote of confidence."

"Sorry, it's obvious that one clown in this room doesn't appreciate me."

"So what!" I said raising my voice slightly.

"So plenty," he said, "that's it! I've had it with this club. Let's go to the Museum of Art."

"Museum now, at this ungodly hour? Are you crazy?" I said.

I added, "Old Man Winter's icy fingers will smother the fifty miles of black ice-covered road leading to the city. We don't need to perform automobile figure eights on those gut-wrenching streets." He won the argument. Our car sledded and glided toward the city's glitzy webs of light like a seasoned Mambo dancer. Eventually, after a thick, swirling fog of flurries persisted in boogieing off the windshield, I said, "You do realize that the museum is closed." His lips pursed.

I babbled, "Milano, where do you suggest we sit when we reach the museum?"

"Relax," he responded with a Dean Martin type of compo-

F. Anthony D'Alessandro
Celebration, FL

sure, "we'll snatch that shovel you carry in your trunk and clear the steps of winter's cold, wet blanket."

"Okay, let's shovel the stairs and sit on the cement steps outside the moat hugging this Fort Knox of art," I said while his eyes danced and his smile stretched from ear to ear.

Fresh sprinkles of snow stalked us, seeming to cover and caress the highway throughout our drive to the city. After our arrival, Mike acted like a Jack-in-a-Box. He frantically cleared a dry spot on the library steps. Mike paused and pointed at a furrowed man sporting a long, Santa-like beard. He said, "Look at that lucky grandpa crouching in the shadows with his towheaded grandson at this hour?"

"In this weather and at this time, it seems like child abuse," I said.

Milano rotated his head side to side vigorously in disagreement. Suddenly, he dashed, slipping and sliding toward the curb, reached out like a football defender and snatched the running boy before he slid into a moving taxi. I heard a thud and noticed a red fluid seeping from my pal's right knee, obviously a result of Milano's crash into the taxi. He'd saved the boy's life. Seconds later, the hobbling and wheezing grandfather stumbled onto the scene and squeezed the boy as tightly as pro wrestlers bear hugging each other. He squeezed Mike too. The grandfather and grandson turned, waved and left immediately.

I offered to clean Mike's bloody knee with my car's first aid kit. He refused loudly and suggested, "Let's reminisce about our informal acquaintance growing into friendship after our boss offered me the part-time job as your photographer. We interviewed well-known *literati*, politicos, and athletes. Titles, degrees, crowns, country clubs failed to impress us."

We joked about our recent encounter with a famed athlete at a restaurant. The man's name appeared in the press more than the president's name. Mike bluntly said to the jock, "You some kind of athlete, ballplayer, or something?"

F. Anthony D'Alessandro
Celebration, FL

Obviously, he remained unimpressed by celebrity. I teased Mike about the new part of his anatomy, his digital camera. I wondered aloud," Is that camera attached to your body?"

"It's about quality of this camera."

Mike seemed to converse with his fancy camera and wore it like an extra appendage. I told him about my appreciation for his photo time ritual. First, he fiddled with the lens, then twisted and turned knobs of the camera, moved boldly toward the subject's face, finally commanding, "Turn your cheek! Head up! Other side, this one is too ugly." These celebrities always laughed. For some reason his sarcasm, smirk, and demeanor never offended them. He possessed a strangely gruff, yet uniquely charming manner.

Milano was a Renaissance man. In addition to English, he read Latin, and spoke Greek, Italian, French, and Spanish. He chatted intelligently about a multiplicity of topics. I heard him explain aspects of DaVinci's submarine to a boat designer. The boatman's mouth remained agape throughout the explanation. He fluidly cited Machiavelli to politicians. His explanation about the physics of a curve ball to a college baseball coach fascinated me most.

Little slipped past the filter of Mike's awareness. One day while we interviewed one of the major surviving novelists of the past century, that writer's twenty-five year-old son strolled into the den with his date. All three of our heads spun as furiously as the crazed dolls appearing on Friday night horror movies. *Surely, I'd seen the son's friend on some modeling runway*, I thought.

"That's great," said the seasoned writer after the young couple excused themselves. Milano noticed the wrinkled writer wiping his brow with a well-used handkerchief, simultaneously gaping at his son's slithering companion. Mike continued, "Sir, you stared at that woman like an opera devotee would have gawked at Pavarotti." Without skipping a beat, the furrowed scribe said, "Women are divine to me. What else is there? Then, your son turns out like you and it

F. Anthony D'Alessandro
Celebration, FL

eats your heart out when he brings them home." I told the scribe that I hoped that we'd have his fire in our septuagnarian years. "My gosh, Petey, when that seasoned writer spots beautiful women, he seems to drool more than a teething baby. Interesting man," said Mike.

The previous week after interviewing a coughing, sniffling politician who continually ran the back of his hand across his dripping nose, while a pyramid of soaked tissues sat scattered on his end table, Mike said, "Pretty sneaky Petey, I'm the only polite one on our team. I'm the one who was exposed to pneumonia. Right?"

"What are you talking about?" I asked.

"You saw our tottering, ailing host sneeze all over the herb tea he served us. I drank mine. You, on the other hand, stealthily poured yours into the sink after the sneeze. I might add that you waited until the man was looking away from you. You never even sipped it." He paused then added, "When we walked into his dirty office and stood for a moment, waiting for the host, you said, 'We should have brought those plastic foot baggies and wrapped them around our feet and legs.'" As I said, little slipped by Milano's filter.

In Mike's company Picasso, Leonardo, and Pirandello assumed a vibrant new life. His words laced around me and opened thought filled pathways. Dumas lived again. They all spoke thru my buddy's velveteen voice. I never learned more in a college classroom. I was never more inspired at a writer's conference. I never gained more insight from the Great Books than from listening to Michelangelo Milano as he spoke while riding in my Austin Healy as we rumbled toward numerous assignments while our helpless hair blew and flapped like flags in a hurricane.

Then, on blustery late December day, draped by a curtain of black clouds, we waited outside our interviewee's home for the gates to open. Mike blurted and poured out his heart. He sliced at my soul when he said, "Petey, I'm a murderer!"

My face froze. My lower lip trembled. How does one react

F. Anthony D'Alessandro
Celebration, FL

to that? Finally, I grudgingly questioned, "Is this your idea of a sick joke or something?"

"I'll bet you never knew that your buddy could kill," he said while biting his nails.

I pleaded, "Cut it out Mike. You're scaring me. Stop foolin' around!"

He paused, "Ever notice my limp? Sure you have. Everyone has. You were just too polite to ask about it. Wanna know how I got it?"

He gazed up at the heavens and continued, "Some drunken Nazi bum shot at my leg. Almost lost it too."

"Sorry Mike, you never told me about that."

"Petey, I'm not begging for sympathy here!"

Milano steamrolled over my scattered reaction and pushed on with his tale. "Toward the end of the Nazi occupation of Italy, I was fifteen and joined a renegade cleric in our underground. We euphemistically referred to ourselves as Freedom Fighters. Obviously our choice of name was not too original nor creative. We were, however, skilled killers. We assassinated scores of Nazi soldiers in Northern Italy."

I interrupted, "Mike, that's war. They were an occupying army."

"True Petey, but many a night I sniped at unarmed German soldiers who were simply walking and chatting."

"Just the same. They were Nazis, and those were simply the scars of war."

Milano said, "I discussed art and artists several times with one of my victims. Just days later, I shot him in cold blood. With raised brow and proud wink, that soldier once showed me sketches he'd made of his family. The man was an artist too. When he heard my name was Milano, he said, 'Many Italian Jews took on the last names of cities.' "

Mike paused, mopped his forehead with his right hand, and pulled out his Star of David necklace from under his shirt. He placed it in the palm of my left hand. Milano continued, "Surely an artist must have noticed this star under

F. Anthony D'Alessandro
Celebration, FL

my shirt. Defiant and proud I still wore it under several layers of shirts. The Nazi artist's eyes and body language telegraphed that he'd spotted it. I thought I was a dead duck. I sweated for several days. The soldier never reported me. Obviously, he didn't share that information with anyone."

Mike rubbed his eyes and he continued, "The German draftee didn't want to be there. That soldier-artist opened a faded book of photos and smiled proudly when showing me beautifully chiseled faces of his three ebony haired non-Arian looking children. The fellow artist told about dreaming about holding hands in prayer with his family in Germany again and of drawing, painting, and sculpting them, too.

That Nazi soldier confided in me, "I am so afraid that Hitler will order us to destroy your city's art. I honestly don't know how I'd react to that." The Nazis forced him into a low level clerk's position in that cursed army. He wasn't a killer. I was! I murdered another artist in cold blood. I saw him in that dammed evil uniform and I went crazy one night. Pop! Pop! Pop!"

"Proud to be my friend now? Right? Do you hate me, fear me, or both now?" said Milano.

"None of the above. I was thinking about my younger days."

I hesitated and added, "I really don't feel like reliving that right now but, in fairness to you, since we are sharing," I added, "my mind frequently forces me to visit the hard concrete sidewalk near Sheepshead Bay. I look down on the freckled and pale eighth grade boy lying motionless at my feet. I kneeled, gently slapping his face while I prayed for his life. In a moment his eyes flutter. My fight seemed legitimate, the older bully shoved me first. Somehow, my usually somnolent sucker punch buckled the boy to his knees and then delivered him to dreamland. My prayers, begging for the boy's life were answered."

Soaking up tears, I said, "The Lord handed me a second

F. Anthony D'Alessandro
Celebration, FL

chance. Mike, with gun in hand, you did not share my good fortune. You proved more effective and your adversary died."

Milano took a deep breath and said, "I killed many, yet the only one that continues to haunt me is that artist and his startled face. When I shot him, I remember his glaring at me with a wrinkled forehead expressing bewilderment and betrayal. A pained tooth grinding look that I'll never forget. His agony still haunts me."

Milano cradled his face in his visibly clammy hands and said, "I felt the pangs of an artist unfulfilled, thought of a screaming widow, fatherless youngsters, and an ordinary soldier with too many canvases left unpainted, too much abandoned unshaped marble, and a ton of promising talent and dreams callously extinguished. I felt the temporary torment of incomplete creations, the ache and agony of an innocent caught up in a bloody tide of sacrilege, sin, and guilt. Those three shots on that fateful day still rattle my head. Every night they shatter my sleep. I became his executioner."

I offered some glib advice. "Since he ran with with riff raff he'd earned the consequences. You're too tough on yourself. Remember, the soldier was a Nazi."

Annoyed, I wondered, what does Mike want from me? I didn't squeeze that rapid-fire trigger during that war. I could not absolve him. Only God could do that. Still, I refused to condemn my friend.

"Mike," I pleaded, "what is it that you expect me to say? That man was an alien warrior and a card carrying member of a murderous gang that scourged our world. You made him pay for their actions."

He rolled his eyes. It seemed as if he must have seen me as a coldhearted weirdo at that moment. He gave me that what-do-you-know-about-anything look? Mike said, "Your attitude disgusts me. After all, you're a native born American. Frankly, you've never experienced that horror. I thank God for that."

I really didn't want to discuss the matter anymore with

F. Anthony D'Alessandro
Celebration, FL

Mike. It felt as pained mentally as walking barefooted over a beach composed of shattered clamshells. Genocide, unjust wars, murder. It was all so ugly, yet my pal Mike had been enlisted as a passionate first-string player.

My mental impotence in that discussion did not sit well with Milano. He'd been wounded by life and I sat speechless. *What kind of friend was I?* I sweated as a sense of guilt trampled across my mind. Draped in a cover of moodiness, Mike suddenly opened the passenger door wide, leapt out of my car, slammed the door shut and began marching into the night until swallowed up by the snow-white landscape. I called him several times. He never turned around. I sat alone in my Austin Healy realizing that he'd been frank and truthful. Sadly, I never saw nor spoke to him again. After he'd poured out his soul to me, I tried to contact him at work and left messages.

In the past, he'd have responded almost immediately. This time, no answer. I called his home. I called his cell phone. He always returned my calls. No return call. In desperation, I wrote a letter. Never answered. A follower of the three contact rule, sadly I felt my buddy struck out by not responding to any of my three reaches. Foolishly, I failed to initiate another contact.

I glared at another copy of the obituary page, wiped some drops off the newsprint and wondered if Michelangelo had finally settled matters with the Bavarian artist, and, most importantly, with God. Taking a final look at the crinkled newspaper, I saw many of Mike's accomplishments posted. Curiously, comments about his wartime Italian childhood, or aeronautical studies never appeared. I rolled that page and my buddy's biography into a tight ball of newsprint and slam dunked it into my pregnant office pail.

Elmae Passineau
Weston, WI

Long Distance

There's a telephone,
   the old-fashioned kind with a receiver
   you hold to your mouth and ear,
   plastic, bright yellow, blue wheels,
   and big green, red, and orange number pads
   that play melodies when they're pressed
It was Lily's when she was two
   she took it apart,
   sucked on the cord,
   poked at the buttons,
   sang along with the songs
She loved that telephone,
   and now, so do I—
   it has a place of honor on my rolltop desk,
   a reminder of my first grandchild
And perhaps a century later,
   it will sit, still intact and loved,
   in a little girl's room in another house,
   and Lily's great-granddaughter
   will push the buttons
   and sing along

Thomas W. Maciocha
Tampa, FL

Did You Ever?

Had you ever, as a child, blinked awake
A fresh day, when the first welcome sense
Was your twitchy nose, dancing
To your grandmother's baking bread?
And you just stayed still, not needing to move.
Not needing anything really, since that bread
In the oven seemed like all that was required
Because it filled you up with bliss?

Did you ever pad down creaky stairs,
Following the scent and see her there,
In her big white apron, blouse sleeves
Rolled up to her elbows,
Wire glasses fogged with flour
Humming a morning song?

Did you ever see your grandmother's laugh-smile,
As the first sight of a new day?
Have you heard the melody of lace-up shoes
Clump across the kitchen floorboards in a
Half-trot,
To you, this not-yet-blemished child,
This center of significance, of care?

And were you so lucky that,
With all of that, the first words you heard that day
Were in her Polish lilt, and without knowing
The exact meaning of the words,
Knew the gloriousness in them?

Have you ever had your face taken into
Floured hands and been kissed,
For no particular reason?

Craig Sipe
Island, ME

Have you ever known such a morning?
Soon Enough

Lady Cat jumps up
on the armchair

stares past my shoulder
to the library door

and the ghost entering
the room

If I looked around this moment
I am sure

there would be no ghost
but there is an image

in the cat's eyes:
some opaque wraith

she has seen
here before

and chose
in her cryptic

cat-ness not to disclose
They must have a deal

the spurious haunt
and she:

Keep the chair guy
in the dark...

...he will know
soon enough

Carl Little
Mount Desert, ME

My Mother and Prayer
After a family photograph

I think it's me seated in the small chair, my feet
not reaching the immaculate carpet,
focused on lining up my fingers
as my mother seated on the bed shows me
the way to pray, her mouth in mid-coaching,
her own lovely echoing pair of hands
upward stretching.

We wear matching white slippers, terry-cloth robes
as if staying at a spa, our hair flawlessly coiffed—
mine, classic rounded towhead cut,
hers, a gentle brunette wave—
facing each other in a bright white room.
You must understand: my father was
an ad man and his pitch is clear:

Wearing these cottony garments could help
mother and child achieve grace.
He wants to get the hands right before
his wife begins to teach the Lord's Prayer,
leading me in my first act of memorization,
"Our Father, who art in heaven" and the rest,
message made possible by the makers of Martex towels.

Polly McGrory
Waldoboro, ME

Brannelly's Irish Tavern

You can tell a lot about people by what they drink. I should know. Twenty-five years behind this bar has taught me a lot about human nature. I got new customers and old customers and sometimes I'll get a fella just passin' through, but I can always peg 'em right off the bat. I know who they are and what they do, where they've been and where they're goin'. The only time I ever got thrown for a loop was that little darlin' Mollie O'Brien.

I figure she was from another planet, one that wasn't as old and tired as this one. Or maybe from a fairy tale—the sweet little princess lookin' for her charmin' prince. I'll never forget the night she walked in here—the place stopped cold. Every head swiveled to look at this luscious little lollipop, all golden ringlets and peaches-and-cream cheeks.

I remember thinkin', "Whoa, honey! Ye've come to the *wrong* place!" Not that this is a dive, mind ye. Brannelly's is a fine Irish Pub, 'tis...nothin' fancy, but clean as a whistle, and we serve a good brew. A shot is a shot here...no skimpin'. And nobody bothers ye. No cops, no bosses, no naggin' wives. But our regular folks ain't what ye'd call the upper crust. Most of 'em have seen better times. But they're hangin' on, and they don't cause any trouble. They're just lookin' for a minute or two away from the heavy burden of reality.

So here she comes, waltzin' in, smellin' a little flowery, a little soapy, and lookin'...well, lookin' *new*. I thought Michael O'Reilly was gonna fall off his stool, I did. Mike is a Guinness drinker—likes his brew hearty and rich, he does. He's a stocky lad, all muscled up from his buildin' all those new houses on the other side o' town. But like they say, an Irishman is never drunk as long as he can hold on to one blade of grass and not fall off the face o' the earth. Well, Mike had an iron-clad hold on that blade o' grass, I'll tell ye. So

Polly McGrory
Waldoboro, ME

Mollie saunters by him, the poor lad, and he doesn't stand a chance. He looked like he was goin' to propose any minute. And I wouldn'ta blamed him either.

She smiled at him for the flattery of his stare. Then she smiled at poor old Mr. Donnelly as he shuffled back from the loo. He stopped dead in his tracks, he did, at the sight of this cotton-candy dream fillin' up the space in front of 'im. Then she flashed that pearly, high-beam smile on me, and roses of Picardy bloomed in my cheeks.

Mollie sashayed up to the bar stool next to Maggie Flaherty. Maggie welcomed her into our little circle with an outstretched hand. Maggie was definitely a lady, quite a beauty, I'm told, in her younger days. But after her husband Seamus died, she was a bit lost for companionship and took to droppin' by for a pop or two. She liked a sip of Port...said it warded off the evenin's chill. Maybe the evenin's ghosts, too, I'm thinkin'. She motioned for me to serve the young lady, and I asked, "What'll ye have, Miss?"

I'd like a Margarita, please," she replied, sliding onto the stool. Now that's a *real* little lady who knows those fancy foreign cocktails.

"What brings you here, dear?" asked Maggie, as we all waited for the reason for her wanderin' in to our humble waterin' hole. She glanced around the room.

"I'm looking for someone," she stated carefully.

Everybody at the bar looked up at that one. Wonderin' if maybe it was *them* she was lookin' for. Much as I liked these folks, I didn't think there was a prince—charmin' or otherwise—in this motley group. Paddy Flynn was starin' at the soccer matches on the telly. He was a draft drinker anyway...he'd never make enough money to keep this little hothouse flower happy. And she sure didn't look like the diaper/dishwasher type to me. Sean Conroy was watchin' Mollie's every move as he sipped on his Jameson's Irish Whiskey. Sean liked the good stuff, but he was a bit of a rake with the ladies. We were still hearin' stories about how he fid-

Polly McGrory
Waldoboro, ME

dled around with Katie Kilduff and left her with a broken heart and a bouncin' baby boy. I didn't think he'd get that close to our little Snow White here. She seemed to be dancin' to a more liltin' tune than Sean's silly whistlin'..

I figured heaven would've kept an eye on her. Most likely they'd assign her a high- rankin' guardian angel, and he'd be packin' a Smith & Wesson.

Jack O'Brien sat quietly at the far end of the bar. Jack used to be a fine picture of a man, goin' to law school, headin' for the Big Time. But turns out he liked dry Manhat- tans better than dry old law books, and so the only bar he ever passed was right here into Brannelly's Tavern. He wound up in insurance, and folks said it was a sad waste of a bright mind. But Jack was good at it, charmin' the worried Irish housewives out of a few dollars of their husbands' skimpy paychecks, just in case they got lucky and the lads prematurely entered the ranks of the "dearly departed." Then Jack had the happy task of deliverin' the life insurance checks that bought those poor girls a small taste of freedom.

I liked Jack—he brightened up the place with his sparklin' wit and his gentlemanly way of speakin'. But the divil had it in for Jack. The one day, years ago now, that he came in, I noticed that he'd brought his little girl with him, but left her in the car while he came in for a drop. She sat quietly in the car readin' her book, occasionally lookin' out the window to see when he was comin' back. She didn't look bored at all, no...she looked like she knew her place. Well-trained by those nuns at St. Joseph's to sit quietly, be obedient and trust her dad to do the right thing. Well, Jack stayed a little too long that day. There was an accident on the way home. Nothin' serious, but the little darlin' broke her arm. Mary O'Brien bought her daughter all kinds of dolls and ice cream to fix that hurt, and then promptly threw Jack into the street. He's never been the same. Never said nothin' about it, not for the last 15 years, but there's somethin' melancholy tuggin' at the corners of those dark blue eyes.

Polly McGrory
Waldoboro, ME

Maggie says he's an alcoholic, but I still treat him like a good customer.

Well, weren't we all taken by surprise then when our lovely young lady spots Jack way off in the corner and says, "Oh, I think that's him!" Maggie shot me a daggered look clearly intended to seal my lips. I had a hard time with that. Here's our sweet little lass, can't be a minute past 21, and she's headin' for a dead end. I checked Jack out of the corner of me eye. Well, sure I admit he's still pretty good-lookin, but he's halfway into his customary evenin' haze here, he's twice her age, and I don't think he's a worthy candidate for the position of Handsome Prince.

But somethin' in our little lady's shinin' face stops me from blurtin' out the awful truth about Jack. She's lookin' at him like he's a long-lost dream, like she's been lookin' for him forever.

She slowly walked over and sat on the stool beside him, and ye coulda heard a pin drop—we weren't so much as breathin' for the suspense. Jack looked up at her, his eyes a bit hazy, and tried to focus on this unexpected angel. She put her hand on his shoulder and smiled at him. She could tell by the blank look in his eyes that he didn't recognize her. So she helped him see.

"Hey, Dad...It's me...Mollie."

Mary Ann Bedwell
Grants, NM

The Basketweaver

She sits in the dirt, in the shade of the *ramada,*
Reeds and fibers by her side:
Devil's claw, yucca, willow, red willow and skunk weed.
Anyone watching might think her asleep—
Her eyes seem to be closed and her hands move
        rhythmically,
seemingly without conscious thought.
Watch closely, though; you will see the pattern develop
Under her hands.
It might be checker-board or coil, herringbone or twill.
But she is not working under the discipline of pattern or
        design—
She is seeing under the surface, seeing the figures
That will appear on the finished basket.
She may sit there all day, unconscious of the passing of the
        hours.
A conduit between the finished basket
and the reality it contains.

Someday a collector may examine it,
Looking for a clue to its provenance.
Did it sit on the hearth, holding the family's grain
Or was it an offering itself?
What was the inspiration for the figures,
Worked patiently into the weave?
We will never know, can only imagine her purpose
and inspiration.

Kathleen Guler
Steamboat Springs, CO

The Winter Kings

The land sleeps
wrapped in indigo cold
and sightless solitude
in the barren nighttime of the year,
crackling ice the only sound,
plumes of breath unseen,
the smell of cold on Midwinter Eve...

At sunset, the measure of the day's end
and the beginning of the next,
the Holly King's bitter cold laugh
haunts and howls—a lonely sound indeed.
His waxy green leaves and brilliant red berries
Rattle with his defiance.
He holds up his lantern, shows off his catch—
he has stolen the last of the light of the world.
With the roar of his laughter still in our ears,
he rides off on his stallion of darkness.

We've dressed in evergreen and scarlet,
Decorated the houses with sprigs of yew and pine,
to honour the gods, the spirits of the ancient ones.
Since *Nos Galan Gaeaf* —
the new year of the ancestors —
we've drawn deep within
the nourishment of home and hearth
just as the sun has withdrawn into its winter burrow —
In observance we snuff out the hearths,
the rushlights, the lanterns, one by one,
until the last is gone.
And in the hours of the absence of time,
We wait, huddled in the uncertainty of the dark.

Kathleen Guler
Steamboat Springs, CO

Outside,
the snow drifts in whispers:
he is coming,
he is coming...
Children whimper, their mothers hush them,
Fathers watch,
Waiting, waiting...
Will he? Will the Oak King come?
Will he defeat the Holly King and break the grip of winter?
He always has, since time out of mind.
But what if he cannot this one time?
Will we live in darkness forever more?

Across the frozen ground,
blown like ice on the colorless wind,
shadows stir like feathery gauze.
Through air knife-edge sharp with cold
the silence cannot be more complete.

Then,
as the midnight call echoes from rampart to watchtower,
a single sparkle begins across the night sky.
The Dragonstar—whispers haunt from the houses—
It streams golden fire-ice
a shimmering messenger
of Light
of Magic
of Miracle
and in a crystalline shower,
the Oak King bursts forth from the woods on his white stal-
lion.
Into the center of the houses he races, to a pile of wood set
high.
 "Here is the light of the world!" he shouts,
and he sets his torch to light the wood.

Kathleen Guler
Steamboat Springs, CO

Cheers rise;
in every home, hearth after hearth is rekindled.
The music begins.
We dance in rows and circles, sing, give gifts of sweets.
In a flurry of leaves,
the Oak King spreads acorns across the frozen land.
The Wheel of Time has turned—
the bounty of summer is on its way again.

***

Andrea Suarez-Hill
Jonesboro, ME

Beach Day

Waves' white water
gift grey after grey
sea to beach,
manes and tails
above Earth's reach

Comber after comber,
salt air rings with
hooves in harmony,
muscles flexed, sinews stretched,
carved and blessed

Each breaker borne equus
roils with joy whilst
from ocean to sand
broad backs swing
and reins go slack.

John T. Hagan
Springboro, OH

Of Running

I have always been a runner. Even as a child, something about running from one place to another made an otherwise entirely mundane or humdrum errand more of a majestic quest than an ordinary task. The delicatessen near our home often became my strategic objective in a Pony Express-like run down the alley behind our home and across Emerson Avenue whenever my dad commissioned me to rescue a loaf of bread and a half-pound of cold meat. He and my mother would be home for lunch from nearby workplaces. I would set my own bar for the speediest roundtrip, easily fudged to establish a new personal best. During one such mission, in pursuit of my all-time record, I dropped and stepped upon the loaf in a swift but involuntary movement that left my parents with mangled bread slices that I argued, acting as my own attorney, were in a corrupted condition at the time of purchase.   For me, delivery speed always trumped product quality and steadfast honesty.

Any footrace distance became an epic event. Using the city transit buses for school transportation as a youth, my disembarkation each day from my yellow limousine on Catalpa Drive made the short, potholed block of Shelton Lane to my home on Rugby Road an exhilarating release from seven hours of stringent strictures under the nuns of my Catholic grade school. The run from bus stop to home was my training for the gold medal I would win one day in the 100-meters at the World Games or Olympics held in some exotic, foreign venue. I would invariably nip my closest competitor at the finish line (my front yard), and he, of course, would be a Russian, the end of World War II and the Korean War setting the stage for Cold War dramatics performed by schoolboys of my era.

My grade school playground provided myriad opportuni-

John T. Hagan
Springboro, OH

ties to exhibit the state-of-the-art advances of my high-top Keds or Red Ball Jets. Several games or activities showcased my foot speed, but no blacktop play was more to my advantage than gang tag. The game placed no restrictions on participants, but they were typically of the same grade level. The object was to be the last man standing or to survive until the outdoor bell summoned us from recess to the rigors of dividing fractions, multiplying decimals, or that torment inspired by the Spanish Inquisition, diagramming sentences. (Only the ignominy of laboring in solitary confusion at the chalkboard over a math calculation exceeded the humiliation in the same situation while pondering the placement of an angled or vertical line to identify the subject, predicate, or complement in a sentence-parsing crucible.)   Until the dreaded bell ended my daily "fifteen minutes of fame," my running skills kept me in the sheer delight of an artful dodger frustrating his most dogged pursuers.

As a high school freshman or sophomore, returning from a nighttime event on the city bus that was for me becoming an embarrassing mode of transport, I would exceed the foot speed I achieved as a grade school kid traversing the distance from bus stop to home, not so much as a challenge or competition but for the fear of what might lurk in the bushes along the ominously dark Shelton Lane.

Although my foot speed never impressed the coaches of athletic teams at my huge all-male high school, it did serve as a kind of vindication of my non-varsity-letter status. After four years of maddening rejections in tryouts for the football, baseball, and basketball teams, I had one last chance to establish athletic prowess. As my school had yet to implement a formal track team, the closest facsimile at that time was the annual all-school track and field meet, commenced in the previous May of my junior year. Having every intention of competing in the inaugural event at a nearby sports park after classes, I was withheld from participation by my math teacher who demanded that I remain at school that day

John T. Hagan
Springboro, OH

to complete a delinquent homework assignment from the previous week. As a result, my first opportunity to participate in the meet was in May of my senior year. Having submitted three allowable competition choices on the requisite form to the Athletic Office a week in advance, I was set to run the 50, 100, and 220-yard dashes.

On the day of the competition, nearly every football and baseball speedster was assembled in what was expected to be a contest of swift-footed running backs, wide receivers, and outfielders. The long and short of the day is that after two or three heats in all three of my races, I dusted the luminaries in the finals of each to post wins in the 50, 100, and 220-yard dashes. The awards for the seniors were made at the baccalaureate breakfast, and I glowed privately as I approached the speakers' table to accept their congratulations for each victory. Did that day expunge the heartbreak of my rejection from every athletic team? Empathically, no! It did, nevertheless, underscore the debatable judgments of a seemingly organized predisposition among certain coaches.

After college and in the course of a career as a high school teacher, I began distance running, purely for the exercise and the aerobic benefits. In time, I began running the middle-distance 5 and 10K races and found that while I would never win races of such lengths, I would often place in the top five or ten contestants in my age groups. As I progressed as a distance runner, I began to experience the so-called "runners high" attendant to the glow of sweat and exhaustion after a formal race or a taxing run on neighborhood streets, a sandy beach, a mountain road, or any vacation scene blessed with natural beauty. Running 3-5 miles allowed me to settle into a stream of consciousness that summoned old relationships, professional experiences, sublime moments, and a host of other memories otherwise buried in the back country of my psyche.

In my advancing years, running helps sustain my will to live as an animated human being. If an ailment or an infir-

John T. Hagan
Springboro, OH

mity even temporarily interrupts my running regimen, I become depressed and crestfallen. Seeing younger runners out on the street in virtually all kinds of weather imbues me with the resolve to keep pace; to eschew the comforts of the warm room and soft couch. I freely admit to feeling superior to the sedentary or corpulent souls my age or younger whose idea of physical taxation is golf-cart driving, Wednesday-night bowling, or mixed-doubles tennis. I also freely admit that I believe I can still keep pace with shapely female runners wearing braided ponytails, designer ball caps, and pastel Spandex (or at least keep them in my line of vision). Nothing revives my fading energy and resolve like the sinewy legs and arms of an agile woman crushing a steep mid-race hill or unleashing a slashing kick to the finish line of a 10K race. She is the same woman who sweats instead of perspires.

As a child I was prone to walking on my tiptoes, and I have heard numerous theories as to what physiological condition that suggested. It was not a conscious thing, nor did it serve any purpose, but I am of a belief that it was an early indicator of my being prepared to break from a starting line that might lie anywhere in my path. Perhaps it was part of a primordial instinct to catch the prey or flee the predator. It may also have portended my intolerance for protracted school studies in a fixed condition. I do not know. What I do know is this: running has been integral to my *raison d'e-tre.* I hope that when I've finally "shuffled off this mortal coil," I'll be "laid to run" in baggy shorts and Shoe-Gooed Reeboks.

Tammi J. Truax
Eliot, ME

Cutting the Roots

I moved the lilac tree again.
The one from the house we shared
that I dug up, panting and cursing,
and placed near your grave
so you'd feel at home.

Only it thrived
over this last decade
gaining strength every year
until the gravedigger said
it had to go.

So I wrestled it home,
alone, again,
and reinstated it
next to the back door
of my new house,

so that maybe, finally,
I might feel at home.
First we'll have to see
if we survive another
shock to the tired roots.

Only time will tell.

Alice Bingham Gorman
Spruce Head, ME

A Poem Comes

A poem, like love,
comes unbidden,
a surprise gift,
a flash of green
in an arc of sunset.

The moment it appears
I must accept it.
If I hesitate, it will disappear
beyond the horizon,
lost to me forever.

***

Encounter at Hannaford

We stood in front of the napa cabbage,
her cart bumping into mine,
her smile, a flicker of times past,
of summer sailing, free spirits,
rum and tonics at sundown.

How are you? I asked.
And you? she said. It's been too long.

For years we didn't speak:
family splits, letters of vitriol,
law suits over property.
Who's allowed to play tennis
or use the family dock?

Alice Bingham Gorman
Spruce Head, ME

How is it living alone? she asked.
My cart nearly empty,
my husband so recently gone.
Mine's gone too, she said,
although we never married.

I'm sorry, I said, eyeing
her chicken sausage and sprouts.

And your brother? I asked. Has he recovered?
His liver tumor's still there
but he's back to drinking rum.

We spoke of her mother, her memory loss,
all gone but the distant past.
Like us, I thought, the short term gone,
property issues settled.
We stood together, all smiles,
old friends picking up the past,
strangers sidling around us,
picking up broccoli and beans.

MJ Herrling
Bradley, ME

Finding Kinship at Winter's Edge

Toadstools shake their fists
at first jut
of winter's breath rising
in the valleys of the night.

Washington's soldiers ease
from catacombs,
beneath my great aunt's
Bosc pear trees,

bones smelling
of old white wash,
limbs snapping
like dry muskets.

My sister-in-law keeps
her pot-bellied pigs, each,
in its own corral beneath the stair
where she rubs them every night

with comfrey and myrrh.
At winter's edge,
we grasp summer's last
incandescent dreams

blazing forth
like Bach cantatas
violet to red,
blue to indigo

Genie Dailey
Jefferson, ME

Under the Big Top

All it took was a wobbly card table and an old blanket, and we were transported to a secret world—right in the middle of our living room. It didn't matter what color the blanket was (though my favorite at the time was blue); once my sister and I were ensconced beneath its card table gables, the world outside disappeared.

Whispers, giggles, and muted kid arguments ensued when we were surrounded by the wooly drapery of our makeshift indoor tent. We played Candy Land or Go Fish or Old Maid, and let the rainy or snowy outdoor world pass us by. Our living room tent could make the worst day into one of the best. It was magical.

Not so magical was the *real* tent my family had when we were older. It was a monster—nine by twelve feet in size, and complete with a ridgepole about seven feet above the floor. It also had an attached canopy on the front that provided shade and a dry place—well, semi-dry—for a couple of folding chairs and a small table for the Coleman stove. These were the *good* features. The *worst* thing about it, though we didn't know any better back then, was that it was all canvas. It probably weighed in at forty or fifty pounds when it was dry. Add to that the weight of the steel poles—none of this modern aluminum or fiberglass stuff—and all our other camping gear and suitcases, and the rear of the station wagon was riding low.

Imagine, then, how the rear end of the wagon felt when we had to load up a *fully-saturated* monster tent at the end of a memorable trip to Nova Scotia. That was a ten-day vacation during which there was only one sunny day. The rest of the time, it was either fog soup or serious drizzle. Everything that wasn't actually wet was the definition of clammy—right down to our shoes and pillows. And the watchword in the

Genie Dailey
Jefferson, ME

tent was "Don't touch the canvas!" If you did, the water on the outside would bleed through, and a continual leak would result.

On the up-side, once my sister and I had learned the mechanics of putting the poles together, positioning them in the grommets, and raising and staking this canvas cabin, the two of us could put that sucker up in twelve minutes flat... when it was dry, that is. When it was wet and had to be dried out...well, that wasn't so easy, and probably accounts for my sister's present-day preference for the Holiday Inn.

***

Sylvia Little-Sweat
Wingate, NC

Centurion

Daddy, yesterday on your birthday
I woke to the truth of relative time:
since your death a quarter century
ago, I have been counting down

to mine. What legacy did you leave
behind? Bones stowed in a grave,
tranquil as dusk; trust in a woman's
fidelity and love, never betrayed;

a bloodline to two. Did you imprint
a double helix of felicity, too, and,
despite all of life's importunities, a
lightness of touch as abiding as dust?

Earl E. Weigelt
Winslow, ME

Hail, Wollemi

What manner of survivor is this?
Rooted Signpost Holy Reminder
in a forgotten and tempestuous wild eons
hidden old as dirt quite
literally

descendants long dead
and gone themselves unmet by eyes
scrutinizing and measuring
first among firsts
better companion to behemoth
and leviathan than to millennials
snapping selfies

the first wind to stir your branches
no doubt His own
as over the dark deep
brooded the Ruach
millennia no better than
milliseconds to
Him

and you and i
we stand small beside
and yet more precious still
than this most ancient
pine

A. McKinne Stires
Westport Island, ME

Forever the Other

With our ripped roots bleeding,
we lick our cowardly pride.
We are wall builders,
gate builders, lords of words,

our oppressed thoughts hidden
behind barriers of babble,
our ancestor's rusted nails welded
for locks and iron fences.

We are forever the other color
in our sea of fear and pride
where blame holds the poker
and dominion fans the fire.

Will you ever see a person
in the place where I stand?
Will you always see the other,
won't you trust who I am?

We forever will be slaves
to our senses and their muses,
until our words can be trusted:
fences flattened into bridges.

Donna Bruno
Ft. Lauderdale, FL

Friday Nights With Granny

Most people, including youngsters, look forward to weekends as a respite from work or school—a time to relax, sleep a bit later in the mornings, or share time with family and friends. When I was growing up in Bristol, RI, Friday nights spent with my grandmother were my favorite. Friday night was also "date night" for my working parents; while they were dining or dancing, Granny and I went to the movies.

At the end of the school day, I would walk along stately High Street to her house, a three-story Federalist where she would be awaiting my arrival with a delicious homemade snack. Soon we would be planning the entire evening stretched out before us. First, we would scan the local newspaper, looking for films featured that week at the Pastime Theater, which was within walking distance. In fact, everything one needed—the church, pharmacy, doctor's office, grocery market, schools—were accessible by foot. After selecting our film and putting something good to simmer on the stove, off we would go hand-in-hand, strolling, just as dusk approached, silhouetting our shadows against the massive chestnut trees lining the sidewalk. We weren't actually touching hands, as Granny always dressed in hat and gloves for the "picture show." Invariably the hats, propped on her head, had a small nosegay secured to a filmy veil netting, and with her pearl earrings, she looked very smart indeed. Together we'd hum "Shine on Harvest Moon" or "On a Bicycle Built for Two."

Once we were ensconced within the cinema, the outside world ceased to exist. Sitting mesmerized in the dark, we followed the adventures of Ingrid Bergman and Humphrey Bogart, Jimmy Stewart and Katherine Hepburn, Judy Garland with the Tin Man and Cowardly Lion skipping down the yellow brick road. How we enjoyed those films! On the

Donna Bruno
Ft. Lauderdale, FL

way home, we would chat about what we had just seen.

Arriving home and leaving the New England chill behind us outside, we would be enveloped by the flavorful warmth of her heavenly "Italian Wedding Soup." As I sat down at the sturdy oak kitchen table, Granny proceeded to ladle out a bowl of steaming soup for each of us, garnishing it with imported Parmesan cheese and augmented by crusty Italian bread. The garlic and parsley and chicken flavors wafted around my head as I bent to savor this hearty treat.

Then, it was bedtime. I still recall the most satisfied feeling, being tucked in and nodding off to sleep with the most romantic fantasies swimming in my head—me replacing Ginger Rogers as Fred Astaire's dance partner; gracefully diving from high places like Esther Williams, and best of all, being carried up the majestic Southern Colonial staircase at Tara in the arms of Clark Gable. FRIDAY NIGHTS WITH GRANNY WERE THE BEST!

***

Irene Zimmerman
Greenfield, WI

Oktoberfest

The leaves, except for a few
still in rusty green,
are party-dressed in every hue
from peach to purple to tangerine.

They're hanging loose all over town,
engaged in lively conversations
or simply relaxing as they down
the last and best of sun's distillations.

Jerry James Rempp
Reasnor, IA

If Not for Love

If not for love
why the panting
of the soul?

Why the firefly's
winking if not for
another in the night?

Why the willow warbler's
piping if not for
voices out of sight?

What is pure love
but having a sense
of Heaven's delight—

like awaking gentleness;
first tremors of the soul,
hasty buds in spring snow

What is it to love
and be loved: it is
the end of all things

What is enduring love?
It is the only evidence
of God, desiring no proof

What is man
without love's mantle
embracing him?

Raymond Mosca
Augusta, ME

Passage

The sun's gone down, the lights are out, and the air is cold
The moon is the only thing illuminating my face as I gaze
Out of the second story window onto Bellevue Road
I close my eyes and listen to the ticking of an old
      mechanical clock,
The pulse of the house
Its rhythm is absolute, flawless, only being broken up by
the occasional passing car
I begin to lose consciousness as the hands of time drag me
      into sleep
The hands of the devil are bloody, for God is timeless
As we rest, the hands spin the globe, chain our souls, and
      fray the threads of life
As the road turns from color to black and white
But, in my dreaming, the hands kindle a fire
It is a cool August night
Music echoes through the darkness and The Cape lights up
      with fireworks
As the Roman candles explode in air, I see my grandmother
      smiling
I watch the fire dance, rekindling warm memories
After a long car ride, I see her waiting for me at the door
It's a Christmas party, a Thanksgiving dessert or perhaps a
      Sunday evening dinner
I'm outstretched on the couch early on a lazy morning
These memories are timeless
Realizing the irony of the situation, I regain consciousness
And suddenly thrust into morning
I know now that life is not forever
But maybe, just maybe, love is
Time can be a cruel force

(continued)

Raymond Mosca
Augusta, ME

It marches down the beaten path
With no regard for human life
Destroying anything in it's way
But it also heals
The hands will cut you, make you bleed and leave scars
Eventually, the scars fade
I guess you learn that in 95 years
Where does the love go?
Maybe the sky, or the far side of the moon
Maybe in the changing of the seasons
Maybe in the way we laugh, or the way we treat one
        another
No one will ever know
But there is something that I feel
When all the lights are faded, and I'm at the end of this
        restless road
She'll be at the door like always
Waiting

***

Patrick T. Randolph
Lincoln, NE

Winter Walks with Aylene

Snow on a pine bow;
Silence sings a song with snowflakes.

Father-daughter footprints
        in the snow—

Who's leading whom?

Goose River Anthology, 2018//63

Jon Potter
Rockport, ME

Cole Nuff?

It's sum ole cole, naow, ain' it? Remoinds me some
Of summah; git yuhseff cooled awff et lahst,
Whin I was growin' up, an jumpin' fahst
Roit inta hahbuh watta; then yuh swum.
Thet watta jist abaout wud leave ya numb.
Me an me buddies, we jist hed a blahst.
It's sum ole cole naow, ain' it?

It were them dahm hoat deys, an we was dumb.
It ain' loike naow; that freakin' cole, she's vahst.
Feels loike we was jumpin' in the pahst;
An all thim sweatuhs cahnt defroast ya thumb.
It's sum ole cole now, ain' it?

***

Steve Troyanovich
Florence, NJ

homeward falls the snow

> *Stir the embers: Night is here, the night*
> *that spreads its pulsing web...*
> —Mario Luzi

in the still fall
of snow
trellised darkness
sinks
into the icy bed
of floating constellations
homeward

Goose River Anthology, 2018//64

T. Blen Parker
Richmond, ME

Snippets of Swan Island Life, 1960's

In the summer months, Grampie would be required to pick up groups of visitors at the Richmond State Landing for the Steve Powell Wildlife Refuge Island, transporting them back over in the flat-bottomed, snub-nosed boat named *Swanee* to the Swan Island dock. In addition to being a wildlife refuge, an island legend boasts of an Abenaki Princess named Jacataqua who escorted Aaron Burr on the Benedict Arnold march to Quebec. Often groups of biologists from the State Department of Agriculture would visit with their clipboards and paperwork, leaving with their pictures of deer, fox, ducks, geese or of fields of rye and wheat, or the old homesteads (or architectural elements of them) to take back to their offices. Steve Powell kept meticulous records on these visits following his model for keeping records on the duck and geese population in his biological research.

Grampie tried to follow in those footsteps by keeping his log of daily planting, monitoring and haying the fields and tracking the changing deer population. Boxes of records were handed over from Steve's son, Bob Gleason to Dr. Charles Burden and Richmond historian, Jay Robbins for safekeeping, documenting, and donation to the Maine State Archives in Augusta back in the early 2000's.

During my stay on Swan Island, (named Sowangen by Abenaki natives, later Swango by Dr. Hebbard for his island spa), an old school bus was sometimes used to transport larger groups of people for the tours but normally, visitors sat in the back of the green, flat nosed Jeep on hard wooden benches, bouncing along while Grampie let me give tours of the interesting attractions along the route to the campground. I had heard his narrative of each point of interest so many times I was a fairly good substitute.

Most visitors only stayed for a couple of hours, took lots

T. Blen Parker
Richmond, ME

of pictures, and they wanted to return quickly to predictable civilization. Beginning the tour narrative, I told them about the house with the heavy, hand-carved paneling upstairs, fashioned like the captain's quarters of an old multi-masted schooner. Some of those ships were actually built in one of two shipyards that once existed on the island. One of the thick, dark colored wall panels secretly slid sideways to allow a tightly squeezed three or four people to hide under the eaves of the roof before it is glided quietly back into place. What a mystery all that was for me as a small girl who had not even heard of such things! I had hidden (if only for a moment) many times in the same spot just to see what it might have felt like to be frightened and quietly hidden in there. One house had a hand-painted mural spreading all around the room in a continuous scene of a fox hunt, with dogs, fox, men on horses and lots of willow trees. I could not imagine being quiet enough to remain hidden for very long.

I was told the spot was created to hide women and children from Indigenous attacks but I suspect it might have been utilized during the Underground Railroad days when African-Americans were smuggled up the Kennebec River.

Next stop on our tour was the Curtis Cemetery, where some of the very first settlers were buried. One gravestone, the sole stone listing Perkins as the place of death, belongs to David Reed who died in 1881. We continued onward, stopping briefly for visitors to peer upward to see the huge eagle's nest in a big rotten tree, passed the old corn-crib with it's slatted, outward slanting walls which housed field corn drying for livestock feed in earlier days.

Grampie would stop at the edge of the field where the early Abenaki burial mound exists down by the riverside. In 2010, I appreciated the opportunity to guide historians from Richmond, Dresden, and other historians from the State of Maine who have documented the mound and have now extended trails to the location where they have posted a prayer wreath on the site. The Abenaki burial site is now

T. Blen Parker
Richmond, ME

included on island hiking trail maps, although barely visible now due to erosion.

As the rattly Jeep rolled slowly along the dirt surface of Swan Island's Main Street, my lecture included talking about the blacksmith shop with the huge leather-covered bellows I had explored as a kid when I had a chance. Holding out my hand, I showed the visitors some of the crudely shaped square rusty nails I found made there, surprising them all. I often drew my fingers to my lips making a shhhhhh sound as I pointed to deer standing in the trees, ever so still just off the side of the road watching us as we drove past. Most visitors were excited to realize that the deer had been there all along, or that I had known they were hiding there.

The stained-glass windows with bubbles and other inclusions in the glass windows at the Powell house fascinated me. A vow I made to myself way back then was many years later realized when I relocated to Richmond and opened Reflections of ME, a stained-glass studio on Main Street where I created some of my best windows. American Peace Dove was commissioned by the Maine Veterans Home in Augusta on Cony Road, now a permanent installation in an interior wall. A large depiction of their business logo hangs proudly in Richmond at Innovative Wellness Center in the front window overlooking Route 197. I presented a pegged window frame filled with Dragonflies Over the Kennebec to the Annabella's Bakery-Cafe in Richmond at the bottom of Main Street hill facing the river when they celebrated their first year anniversary. Dragonflies are their business logo and the multi-colored blue and purple background comes alive when kissed by the first magical rays of a morning sunrise. Visitors at the Portland Flower Show saw two of my faerie windows built into a rock wall display in 2010. In addition, my home showcases antique pegged wooden window frames filled with designs taken from nature.

The brick houses on Swan Island were built with bricks from the kiln found farther down the island. A tall brick

T. Blen Parker
Richmond, ME

building named the Hathorn Block on the corner of Main and Front Streets in Richmond still standing today includes bricks made on this island. Les Fossel is in charge of the antique restoration of the building, which he plans to convert inside to condo's and apartments. The birthing chair, which looks like a strange kind of lounge chair sits in the Tubbs-Reed house, and the spinning wheel I played with and several odd rocking chairs are still inside one of the houses. The bust of a woman sits in the window of the Lilly-Wade house, frightening passersby, the piece formerly perhaps guided a sailing ship through salty seas, ending up at the home of Wade men, the craftsmen who built the original Balmy Days in their little boatyard down across the lawn from the house at the Kennebec Riverside.

The Steve Powell house, located where little Swan Island looks near enough to touch, had a special feature in the large farmhouse kitchen called a dumbwaiter. It was a small elevator-type mechanism, which transported food from the kitchen via a square shelf about three feet wide with rope and pulley system. When hand-pulling the rope over the pulley, the shelf, and contents raised trays (somebody's midnight snack or breakfast in bed?) up to a bedroom from the kitchen. Such a unique, clever way to save running up and down the steep and narrow stairway from what might have been the maid or cook's bedroom to the kitchen below. A smaller room next to the kitchen had a solid panel that slid aside something similar to a takeout window used for passing food or drink or empty dishware back and forth to the kitchen. Some of the visitors to the island stayed overnight, camping near the Dumaresque saltbox house in the Adirondack style log lean-tos across from little Swan Island.

Back then, I felt privileged to ride in the cab of the truck with Grampie every day when he made his rounds to feed the deer their supper grain down in the sick pen, located beside the Lilly-Wade house. The area, about a two-acre plot surrounded by a high chain link fence with a gate, was named

T. Blen Parker
Richmond, ME

the "sick pen" being where injured deer were kept until they were well enough to fend for themselves. The pen is also where "Jerry the moose" lived until being shipped in a wooden crate to the Bronx Zoo where he lived until quite old.

The sick pen really gained its name when the State of Maine conducted the caribou project. It was only then (early 1960's) discovered that whitetail deer and caribou do not cohabitate in a healthy way. Wooden crates brought the caribou from Baxter State Park by helicopter, landing at the Swan Island dock in Richmond where they were transported over the river on Grampie's barge. I'm not certain why the helicopter didn't land on the island but suspect it was due to not wishing to cause anxiety or chaos for the other animals. I stood safely out of range, up in the back of the Jeep watching the frightened, wild-eyed snorting caribou being set free in the island fields. When the game wardens first slid the front door of the crate up, the caribou, still timid and shocked by the trip, had to be coaxed out of the crate. As soon as their caribou-eyes got accustomed to the natural light, they hesitated enough to sniff the island air then sprinted off, leaping high across the field. The deer they came in contact with first made them very sick, eventually killing them all off completely due to a parasite.

The narrow, winding dirt road was lined with cedars and evergreen trees. I saw so many types of mushrooms and green moss covering the roadside, the forest seemed enchanted to me. I carefully made fairy-houses there by the side of the road while waiting for Grampie one day. On our very next trips down the island, I couldn't help admiring them, thinking that I had secretly prepared houses for those wee forest fairies to stay dry on rainy days. Probably the idea of tiny folk came from hearing stories of leprechauns while visiting my Irish Gramie Molly, who lived in an apartment in Gardiner.

Years passed until this particular day, my face turned into the chilly wind, tightly closed eyes, I pulled the red shawl

T. Blen Parker
Richmond, ME

around my shoulders that grandmother had crocheted. Gramie would have loved to see me still wearing it today. My mind is flooded all at once with memories of the loneliness I thought as a child, was "the pits." There were happy times, as well. I learned to read by using Reader's Digest as a text-book, learned to cook in a woodstove oven, learned the proper way to wash clothes in a hand-wringer washing machine, mastered swimming without a life jacket in the little frog pond, and learned how to drive on a standard shift vehicle, a one-ton International stake-body truck.

Sitting on my reflecting rock on this day, these thoughts raced through my mind as fast as my heartbeat. Slowly, a smile kissed my lips and I was swept back into the past. I remembered churning ice cream. The sweet smell of Gramie's molasses beans baking in the woodstove oven made me suddenly salivate, the whitetail deer appearing like clockwork at the kitchen window each morning where they patiently waited for the stale bread and potato or apple or carrot peelings I fed them. Scowling, I noticed I was doing it again—that habit of twisting my mouth to the side with the end of my tongue sticking out like a cherry tomato, just like when I did homework by the light of a kerosene lantern at the kitchen table. The memory of a smoky-scented wood fire that I woke up to many mornings flooded my mind like the warm blood in my veins. I had made this very same trek numerous times throughout my childhood—across this matted dry grass, through the blueberries, across the field to sit on my reflecting rock.

The tiny cars were still there, like so many times before but on a different bridge then. I imagined they would still be filled with tiny people, just outside of my reach, crossing the green swing bridge that connected the towns of Richmond and Dresden. A giggle escaped just for the moment as I remembered the crazy game where I pinched the tiny cars between my thumb and forefinger and pretended to pluck them off the bridge to bring over to the island to play. Since

T. Blen Parker
Richmond, ME

the State of Maine took over the island by eminent domain, we were the only family on the island. In those days, I frequently stayed with my grandparents following the doctor's grim diagnosis of a terminal and rare bone disease. My grandparents decided they had more spare time than my young parents to manage my multiple appointments, being able to provide the consistency of nightly olive-oil massages on my brittle knobby hands, elbows, knees, and ankles. They believed they could make a difference in my life, possibly even reverse the calcifying process while on the island. Back in the nineteenth century, Dr. John Hebbard advertised his health resort SWANGO as a healthy, wholesome retreat for people with any kind of illness from melancholy to consumption. Swango was advertised in *Ballou's Pictorial* newspaper in the 1800's. I would not succumb to the disease before the age of ten if my grandparents could do anything to prevent that outcome!

Sitting on the massive rock, I sensed my grandparents' arms engulfing me for just a fleeting but strong squeeze. I envisioned their wry smiles, felt their loving approval of my decision, felt the rapid hummingbird flutter of my heart, and then only calm. Communication felt that way between them, like the warm olive oil massages I received as a child. I knew then that my decision was right; they would proudly approve. Taking a full breath of pure island air, I was filled with hope again and caught myself smiling back at my own strong reflection in the calm water below the rock.

This day I was sitting on my reflecting rock once again, a boulder much larger than a Volkswagen Beetle on the riverside. "How about that!" I thought for a moment, taking in a healthy gulp of fresh air and holding it. "If we had believed the diagnosis when I was three, I wouldn't be sitting here today. I've beaten the odds at least once, huh Gramie?" It was not uncommon for me to speak right out loud to my grandparents or great-grandfather, although I didn't pretend they were here in person. There is a fine line of communica-

T. Blen Parker
Richmond, ME

tion still open between us, like microwaves bouncing off a satellite dish, a sort of spiritual cellphone to the grandparents I feel are responsible for my survival.

I paddled my bright yellow, birthday kayak across the Kennebec River from the Richmond dock to the island on this particular morning. My loving grandparents had long since passed away, but the island is the place I feel closest to them. Whenever visiting this place, I feel their comforting "presence" as strongly as the ray of sunshine that washes over the crown of my once thick auburn hair, now silvery white, shining as brightly as the surface of the water. Sitting there allows me a spiritual experience; I have done it many times, consider it my own form of meditation. Pleased to visit my special place on my birthday, intense thoughts flowed through my mind, churning like the turning tide in the river. Enjoying the eagle's squawk to reprimand their young eaglets, my nose wrinkled at the raw earth scent exposed only at low tide.

Historical research into the families who once lived here has taken many hours, days, weeks, and months, uncovering ice harvesting, shipbuilding, blacksmithing, brick, and glassmaking during the height of Perkins. My journey has taken me to search Maine newspapers, visit archival libraries, attend lectures on the history of Maine, comb through bookshelves lining often hidden, independent bookstores throughout Maine, eventually purchasing books of historic accounts, from before and after Maine had parted from Massachusetts. I regularly pore through ancient, badly handwritten, and faded journals, peruse copies of Plymouth Company letters, sort through pencil sketches or faded black and white pictures.

I am insatiable in my quest. Meetings with historians from Dresden and Richmond, the two towns surrounding the island, are lengthy but ever so beneficial, providing details I could not have otherwise known. Visiting the Curtis Cemetery again provided a photo opportunity of the grave-

T. Blen Parker
Richmond, ME

stones belonging to people whose journals I have read. Richmond's historian hosted a "reunion" of several individuals who had lived on the island. During that reunion, I met the Wade sisters, Josephine and Patricia. Delighted to share several opportunities for lunch or share tea with Wade sisters who lived on the island as young girls, made my summer one to remember. Hearing them recount personal family stories, hearing Jo read from a journal written by a relative about her island experience, precious moments I treasure.

The idea had been incubating in my mind all along; the time to act has arrived! As soon as I returned home that day, I began to write the book I hope will inspire someone to revive some part of the island, perhaps as a wellness retreat or at least offer the history via an on-island information center, my legacy.

NOTE: *Swan Island in The Kennebec—Journey to Sowangn—Island of Eagles*, the first of the Swan Island trilogy novels soon to be published in the fall of 2018 by Maine publisher, **Goose River Press** of Waldoboro. Book launch party (TBA) scheduled at the Lincoln County historic property, Pownalborough Courthouse where John Adams heard cases is just upriver from Swan Island.

Craig Merrow
Wells, ME

Oh Sandy

On the day you were born you stuck your fist in your
        mouth
Your phweeting was the very first sound you made
Such a joyous noise that stole our hearts
But it was your beautiful smile that made our day

Oh Sandy,
You were such a lovely child
And you grew up in such a beautiful way
To grow up with you was so wonderfully wild
But it was the way you touched our hearts that made our
        day

A free spirit with a heart of gold
The crazy things that you did, and nobody told
But it was the way that you helped, and the love that you
        gave
Topped off with a beautiful smile that made our day

Oh Sandy,
Your joy and laughter that you never hid
About all the funny things that you did
When I think of you, I can't help but smile
Because you showed us how to live
And how to make it all worthwhile

You traveled the world to sail and to fly
But when you came home someone special caught your eye
Tall dark and handsome, he asked for your hand
And when you said yes, a new adventure began

Craig Merrow
Wells, ME

Oh Sandy,
From the way Hollis swept you off your feet
To the way you made each other's lives complete
A dashing groom and his blushing bride
You both took to the stars to dance and to glide
The way your spirits soared on that beautiful day
With your hand in his, and you were on your way

Then one day you were gone too soon
We were saddened and at a loss that day
We didn't know what we would do without you
And we struggled with the words we wanted to say

Oh Sandy,
But your spirit still shines through
In our memories of you and in everything we do
You will always be the sun that shines on us every day
It's not about answers, sometimes we just have to believe
And I believe that we will see your beautiful smile again
someday

Dedicated to the Loving Memory of Sandra Sleeper-Cole
May 23, 1966—February 9, 2018
and to the
Rockland District High School
Class of 1984

Robert B. Moreland
Pleasant Prairie, WI

Sky Watcher

He waits, sitting cross-legged in dimming light
upon the breakwater perch facing east,
expectant; warmth of the day radiating
from the concrete. Twilight fading, the first stars
begin to shyly appear. The lake is calm
after the storms. Gentle waves caress the shore
and he adjusts his breathing to their timing.

As constellations pepper the evening sky,
and are mirrored below in the inky
black surface of the great lake, he closes
his eyes to bathe in the peace. A pinpoint then
a silver sliver glows on the horizon.

Light so bright, he squints as the full moon grows,
brilliant orb, decorated with scrimshaw
like etchings; familiar face. Pulse of the waves
quickens as a southeasterly breeze freshens.

Harvest Moon births from the lake, freed to rise
to his sky throne. Ten thousand shimmers ice
an inland sea. The man, in solitude,
hopes never to lose his sense of wonder.

Peggy Trojan
Brule, WI

Hayloft, 1940

When the men had filled the mow
almost to the roof with sweet dry hay,
Lorraine and I dared ourselves
to spend the night.

Brought thick quilts and pillows,
climbed the slippery mountain.
We listened to the night birds,
the small nocturnal animals,
the clinking bell on the lead cow
wandering in the barnyard.
We looked out the huge door,
with its scary iron fork on the pulley,
at the stars and the vast
unknown universe of our lives.

In the morning
we poured coffee from the granite pot
on the wood stove in the house,
feeling grown-up
and kin to pioneers.

First published in *Red Cedar*, 2018

Karen E. Wagner
Hudson, MA

A Winter's Moon

breaks through
scarred landscape below
with deep shadows
that run into trees

under valleys,
mix with darkness of
night's secrets
behind the old barn

over the water well
to reveal the battered weathervane,
and illuminate a patch by the
rundown shed where

a doe stands in perfect silhouette,
her body shaped
by wisps of clouds blown
through the bare brush,

and she paws earth
for sprigs of fresh wintergreen
under a blanket
of newly fallen snow.

Helen Ackermann
Rothschild, WI

A Healing Touch

There is a publication called *Senior Review* that is available at restaurants and grocery stores as well as other places in our area. The February, 2018 issue included a piece by Kelly Atkins of Azura Memory Care of Wausau, Wisconsin. It focused on the heart brain connection. It seems that the heart has its own brain. The heart brain communicates with the head brain to direct feelings and communication. If a family member has some form of dementia, it is good to give hugs and to touch in a loving manner.

I was reminded of a story I heard at a local nursing home. The gentleman, with whom I spoke, told me of his wife who was living in a nursing home nearby. He would visit her as often as he could. She no longer recognized him enough to call him by name but when he reached for her hand, she would squeeze it and he knew that she recognized him then.

The loving pat on the arm, the gentle hug, the arm around the shoulder can enable the heart brain to communicate with the head brain. Is that why Jesus touched others in his healing of them? We have many examples in the Scriptures of Jesus touching those he healed. One that we might be familiar with comes from the gospel of Matthew, Chapter 8: 14-15. "Jesus entered the house of Peter, and saw his mother-in-law lying in bed with a fever. He touched her hand, the fever left her, and she rose and waited on him." Jesus knew the power of touch. It communicated love and compassion. We too can help to heal when we use the power of our touch to communicate love. It might not be a physical healing but a healing of the heart.

Jean Lawrence
Waldoboro, ME

March 28

Today's my birthday; I'm seventy-nine, or as my dad would
      say, "in my eightieth year."
Birthdays are a part of aging, a neat way to keep time.
We all have them: some quiet celebrations, others more
      fun-filled.

For my eighth birthday, a pink and white checkerboard
      cake was promised, but measles struck.
With candles blazing, the cake was carried to my bedside; I
      couldn't even sit up.
I can still see the checkerboard design in a slice of cake,
      But, my memory?
The grey in my dad's hair as the candle flames lit his face is
      most vivid!

A surprise party given by my best friend marked my
      seventeenth.
What began as a heart-throbbing first date evolved into
      dancing, balloons, cake, and ice cream.
It is a high school memory kept tucked away for safe-
      keeping.

With two young sons and my husband cheering, my thirty-
      second arrived with a new bicycle.
Why so special? I'd never had a new bike of my own!
What a wonderful milestone celebration, and I was still
      young enough to ride!

Jean Lawrence
Waldoboro, ME

My fiftieth was marked by my fellow high school
	department staff.
I was surprised with fifty tulip blossoms filling my office
	that morning.
The gorgeous colors expressed the special regard of my
	fellow professionals. What a blessing!

Over the years, the date has been marked by snowstorms,
	Easter, and even national disasters.
Life doesn't wait, and birthdays appear without prompts.
Now, in the winter of my life, observances are quiet, and I'm
	grateful just to be able to celebrate.

I'm struck by Galiani's words,
"The important thing, Madame, is not to be cured, but to
	live with one's ailments."
So, as I begin my 80th year, I resolve to praise life
	regardless of what it brings
And always to look forward to creating splendid new
	memories.

***

Patrick T. Randolph
Lincoln, NE

Grandma Thinking of Grandpa: Summer of '75

Standing at a dark
Almost midnight windowpane,
Smiles stare out into

Some amazingly empty
World where there's nothing but—song!

Goose River Anthology, 2018//81

Pat Onion
Vienna, ME

Botticelli's Annunciation

I've seen this girl before. On sunny days
She jogs the hilly campus path.
In winter storms she soldiers through to class
Holding her deadline-ready brilliant essay.

Gaze level, she hears the words and knows
The angel has just taken away her life
And given it to God. She doesn't think
Hers will be any life she had imagined.

Later they will paint her
Soft pink, half-dopey, pouty, sensual-stupid.

But I, who have watched her running against the wind,
Honor this girl accepting her tough assignment.

***

Robert Erickson
Round Pond, ME

Pictures

My eyes have captured the shoreline soft
And the vast blue sky reeling gulls aloft
The ocean greys deeply following a misty rain
Pictures perfect of the creation called Maine

**Martha Pritchard
Chapman, ME**

An Astonishing Thanksgiving

Always open to the possibility of forces beyond what we see and what we know, I know that guardian angels like Clarence—the one George Bailey encounters every Christmas when I watch *It's a Wonderful Life*—are real. And I have proof.

In October and November of 2010, some spirit or angel was hard at work arranging a Thanksgiving for my mother that was nothing less than astonishing! Of course, none of us knew that this was to be Eva Brabant's final earthly holiday —she died at the good, great age of 82 just four days before her favorite holiday—Christmas. But getting a head start on eternity was the way she was meant to go—a surprise for her, a shock for those of us left behind.

Mom had a thing about having all of her eight children gathered around her in one great celebration. She always said, "Let's have a funeral party while I'm still around to enjoy it. It won't do me any good after I'm dead."

In 2004 and 2008, with three of us living within walking distance of Mom's home, the others followed our youngest brother Christopher's lead and rallied around Mom in those summers in Maine. Mimi, our youngest sister, was missing in 2008 but she had been with Mom for Thanksgiving in Indiana two years before.

In 2010, the out-of-towners got the call for another reunion party. Again Mom went through her "I can't enjoy the reunion after I'm dead" reminder, and again the family followed Christopher's lead. He named the date and Susan and Barbara brought all available members of their broods from Indiana. Elizabeth made the shorter jaunt from Vermont and we all had a week of pure joy.

That summer, Mom was more insistent than ever, though. There was no change in her health, no alarms we

Martha Pritchard
Chapman, ME

knew of. But her preoccupation with her reunion seemed more urgent. Her usual upbeat spirit was noticeably dampened when Mimi, Darrell, and their three children couldn't afford the trip from Kansas. They just couldn't pull that financial rabbit out of their hat. Maybe if they'd make it in September . . . or perhaps Christmas. But we all knew the likelihood of a visit for them was slim.

So what made the summer 2010 reunion call different? I don't know for sure. But for the first year we could recall, Mom didn't plant a garden. Yet she did make applesauce, apple cakes, and banana and zucchini breads for the freezer. She froze heads and heads of free cauliflower a friend offered, and canned green beans and tomatoes. Jelly jars were all filled with sweets as usual, concocted in her broiling kitchen on the hottest days in summer. There were boxes—cases—of Omaha Steaks and other special treats filling her freezer, and thanks to QVC, she'd discovered a wonderful new hot dog to supplement her steak-stash. After surviving WWII and the aftermath in Germany, she always feared starvation, and always made plans for the future.

But Mom tired more easily that year. She'd start a batch of cookies and put some of the dough in the refrigerator to finish later. She hadn't been sick. She'd gone to all her scheduled doctor appointments, including her visits to her eye specialist. She cooperated with those of us who took her to appointments—frequently apologizing for inconveniencing us as was her habit. That never changed.

It must have been September when Elizabeth got it in her head that we should all get together in Vermont for Thanksgiving. Although Jim and I had agreed to drive her, Mom was lukewarm about making that long car trip. Beth kept her ulterior motive a secret until the details were solid. Then she announced that Mimi and her kids would be there. That financial rabbit was going to come out of Beth's hat.

This wouldn't be a simple accomplishment. Beth lives in the Northeast Kingdom of Vermont. After a train trip from

Martha Pritchard
Chapman, ME

Kansas to South Bend, Indiana, for an overnight stay with our sisters Susan and Barbara, the little group would continue by train for more than twenty-four hours to Albany, New York where they'd pick up the van Beth rented for the final leg of their journey—another four hours.

When Mom heard that news, the light in her heart switched on, and for a few weeks all we heard here in Maine was, "When I get to Vermont . . ." She seemed to be saving her strength for that trip.

After her last eye appointment in October, we went to the grocery store, and she waited in the car while I ran in for the few things we both needed. As I drove from the parking lot, the car faced Kentucky Fried Chicken—one of Mom's all-time favorite treats. I put the blinker on and she questioned me.

"I thought we'd pick up some of Colonel Sanders for the whole gang. We'll call Paul and Jack and their families to come over. The giant bucket is on sale."

"No, let's not. I'm kinda tired."

"Okay, then, I'll just get you a small meal. You can always save it for later."

"No thank you, Honey. I just want to go home."

The following week Mom had a marvelous idea of her own! Instead of leaving in the middle of November, she decided that we should leave "a few days early" so she could attend Beth's concert. You see, in addition to being the director of music studies at Lyndon State College, my sister Elizabeth founded and directed the Northeast Kingdom Community Orchestra.

When Mom announced this idea, I agreed that it made perfect sense. "When would we have to leave?"

"Well . . . tomorrow. I'm all packed already."

"*Tomorrow, Mom*?" I wasn't as flexible as I could have been. I thought the idea outrageous and expected Jim to agree with me. On the contrary, all he said was, "I'll go get the car checked over and gas up. Can you throw a clean shirt and underwear in your bag for me?

Martha Pritchard
Chapman, ME

It was that simple for our Jim. Mom said "jump" and Jim said, "Pack my bag."

I went to Mom's to find out how much luggage she'd be taking for the now month-long stay. "Oh, I just have that one suitcase." Okay, here's the bait-and-switch: Mom style … *and a cooler full of steaks and hotdogs, frozen zucchini bread, apple cakes, and cookies. Oh and a box or two of jams, apple-sauce, apple pie filling, and string beans.* She saved that news until the morning of the trip.

I wasn't a bit amused. I'd be seated in the backseat of our small Mariner wagon. And Mom knew that Jim would move heaven and earth to insure her comfort. That was another surprise she saved until Jim had everything in the car. "Jim, do you think I can bring my bedding too? I just hate sleeping on Beth's old mattress."

And of course Jim and our guardian angel figured out a way to get Mom's queen-size memory foam mattress, two feather beds—one for on top, one for under her, and two queen-size QVC Northern Nights feather pillows in the car. (I had never known my mother to be so selfish about her own comfort.) To accomplish that magic, he folded down the large half of the back seat making an L shape for Mom-packing– leaving me the tiny jump-seat directly behind Jim's seat. Jim is tall and his seat has to slide completely back to allow him to pedal.

On road trips I'm the princess! I'm the one who rides in comfort, with pillows, and inflatable neck-cuddle, blankets for under and around my legs! I do NOT ride in the jump-seat! So I pouted through the whole eight hour trip and Jim and Mom had glorious chats between Mom's naps.

Jim drove straight through to Vermont. Mom hated trav-eling, and even though we worried about the circulation in her legs during such long inactivity, it was easiest on her to get it all over with in one shot with lots of rest stops for her to stretch.

Mom spent the end of October, all of November, and the

Martha Pritchard
Chapman, ME

first week of December with Elizabeth in Vermont. She was at peace knitting and listening to her daughter play the grand piano in her spacious, sun-filled living room. Mom was always so proud of her children, and Beth's Steinway was symbolic for her on so many levels; she was reminded of her of her musical father and brother in Germany, and of all the sacrifices she and Dad had made so we could have such luxuries as piano lessons. Music had been the cement that held her German family together during the challenges of two world wars, and it was music that bridged the language barrier between Sgt. John W. Brabant and Eva Poppendieck when they met in 1945.

The highlight of that extended visit, of course, was the Thanksgiving Day celebration. Finally, after four years, she was able to hug her youngest daughter again and become reacquainted with three much-loved grandchildren. Though they had only four days together, Mom's 2010 visits with her eight children were finally complete. She was happy.

After Thanksgiving dinner, each family member was given a piece of paper on which to write what they were thankful for, and after reading it, they tossed it in the fireplace. Mimi retrieved Mom's words from the edge of the fire, and tucked it in her pocket. In our mother's quirky spelling and elegant German handwriting, this treasure survives:

I'm thankful for all the years that I have lived, and all the things that have happened to me that I can tell stories about. I really love it all. I thank God for my children and that they are so good to me.

So ended our astonishing Thanksgiving!

E.M. Barsalou
Kittery Point, ME

In Memory of Times Shared

Just as Dad did, I like to mosey down an old dirt road.
The drive to the swimming hole, a side-tire tracked line,
Through the wooded spine of narrowly unset trees.
A long time not even growing in between forests of
          fathomed majesties.
Way lowed out past the barrens, the tired grey bog rests for
          eternity.
I have seen this, I have felt this.
As it continuously grapples my past with fears of my mind.
Returns me to it now ever so fast.
.....remembrance of our time shared........

***

Sylvia Little-Sweat
Wingate, NC

Audubon Crossing

Meadowlarks weave nests
from the filigree of Spring—
ground themselves to sing.

Wearing camouflage
Mallards leave sheltering reeds—
follow Summer's lead.

Crested Woodpeckers
strike dead trees with beaks like bone—
Autumn's xylophone.

Celine Rose Mariotti
Shelton, CT

Vegas Strong, Vegas Forever

Vegas Strong,
The spirit of that
Place in the desert,
Where the neon lights glow all night,
Where entertainers love to perform,
Where people gamble and sometimes win,
Where people go shopping,
Or go to a spa,
Or to a gourmet restaurant,
It's the place Frank Sinatra and Dean Martin loved,
It's that special place in the desert,
Where you can be up all night,
And sleep in the day,
It's that special place,
Where people are so friendly
And so welcoming,
Where you can just go to
Get away from it all,
And like my Mom always calls it,
It's LaLa Land,
Where you can forget all your cares,
No one can take that specialness away,
All of us who love Las Vegas,
Will help the city overcome
This terrible tragedy.
As Elvis Presley said,
Viva Las Vegas!!!!

Linda Amos
York, PA

Unspoken Words

Sometimes,
       Words don't really matter.
If you love someone enough
       You can feel the caring
You can witness the devotion
       You can something the adoration
You can testify to the Love.

Even if the words are unspoken.

***

Some Secrets

Some secrets, whether large or small,
Are best kept secret;
Carrying them to your grave.
It is called "life baggage"
Best buried with you when you died!

Jim Ostheimer
Rockport, ME

Coming Home

My husband, my dearest Robert,
how I have missed you
since you went to war.
No one to share my love,
to smile when you smile
or absorb my anger when
the children have run wild.

We have prayed for your return,
wept that you stay safe,
felt the need for you,
realized that a father,
a friend, a lover, must not
be taken from us again.

You may have changed
since we parted and so may we.
Please share with us
your shadows and we will
fill your void with the
brightest and the saddest
of our lives since you departed.

Welcome home a thousand times,
dear Robert, my friend.

Mary Ann Bedwell
Grants, NM

Our House

Our house is full of possibilities—
travel books are scattered 'round,
clips of coupons sit on a kitchen window sill.

We have bundles of fabric,
dozens of spools of thread,
bags and baskets of beads.
Seed packets are tucked among gardening tools.

Bicycles, snowshoes and pool cues
decorate our garage,
hiking boots, balaclavas and windbreakers
cram our closets.

Our kitchen cabinets are full of
Bundt pans, cookie sheets and food processors,
our spice rack is a world tour.

Books to read, music to listen to, movies to watch,
questions to ask, conversations to have,
friends to meet.

Our house is full of possibilities.

John O'Kane
San Pedro, CA

Rebirth

She's lying on her back, head propped on a pillow, staring at the crucifix on her bedroom wall, waiting. She found it in the basement yesterday wrapped in yellowed newspaper clippings about the murder of a small child down the street. The sight of it always unsettled her. Her husband used to joke that she must be a Satanist, but she didn't even know what that was. She did believe in something that made it all happen, the immense Beyond that somehow must include her, the triumph of good over bad most of the time. But she took the crucifix down not long after he died some years ago.

She turns away from it, like she's lost a stare down with a more willful mate, feeling its metallic orbs are watching her every movement, when she hears footsteps alongside the house. "How long have I been off in my thoughts," she whispers. She feels a twinge of pain in her stomach, like the mouthing of words in her head had only muted her condition. "It must be Evelyn!"

The footsteps get closer to the back door but no one knocks or enters. She thinks it might be that peeping Tom hounding the neighborhood. She tries to get up and move toward the phone stand but the pain holds her back, confusing her momentarily. As she stretches out her sister appears, braking her momentum. She reverses course and returns to her settled position on the bed, the pain amplifying to near nausea. She faces her sister with an anxious stare.

"What...are you up to? Why didn't you knock? You scared me half to death!"

"I heard something in the bushes...just wanted to... how're you doing, Adele?"

"I don't know if I can do it! What if...I mean why can't I... what is it I have to do?"

"You know what you have to do...we talked about it, read

John O'Kane
San Pedro, CA

the passages in the good book...you understood! What is it now?"

"I don't see...who said that? I can't even really remember. What's this have to do with me? If the Lord loves me wouldn't he want what I want?"

"He does. It's just that He knows what's best...He sees into all our thoughts and actions in ways we can't. He loves us so...He's always looking out for us!"

"But where is he? There are just these faces that don't seem very happy, they never say anything that says they know or like me, just these phrases that don't make sense. They make me feel ashamed!"

She starts to sob in spurts, which become more frequent and fuse into giddiness, like when excess pain suggests ecstasy. They cease in a blank expression.

Evelyn's lost for words. She turns around, stoops slightly over her bag, pulls out a Bible, hesitates and turns around to face Adele. She grasps it like she's afraid someone might take it from her. Adele's stare fills with disbelief. Evelyn continues to brandish the book. Adele looks at it and into her sister's eyes, clueless.

"It's for the children," Evelyn spouts, becoming animated and more confident.

"Who says?"

"It'll be better off...in God's family, protected from our sinful ways. We must repent, find Jesus to..."

"...do what?"

Adele reacts to her own words like they're spoken by someone else, and senses they're too loud. She looks at the ceiling, thinks she hears sounds, and tries to visualize what's happening. She slips into a trance.

"Adele, Adele, come back to me!" Evelyn says, trying to be quiet but also doing what's needed to snap her out of it. "Where are you?"

Adele concentrates hard to stop breathing and convince Evelyn she's hopelessly comatose. But the pain returns and

John O'Kane
San Pedro, CA

makes her twitch uncontrollably. She tries to tune out Evelyn's words, seeing her oldest son wide awake upstairs. The young ones are probably dead to the world. But she hears only ear static. What if he comes down, what will she do, how will she act? As she reaches a painless plateau she opens her eyes to terror on Evelyn's face. Their looks lock and she can't pull away.

As more footsteps appear alongside the house, she jerks her head away from Evelyn and breathes a sigh of relief, catching a glimpse of her distorted image on the dresser's shiny surface. Her relief turns to horror. She shakes her head back and forth, as if trying to foil a mirage, but can't lose this picture. A jolt of pain freezes her stare. She hears faint voices escaping the fuzzy forms they're attached to.

"Calm yourself my child," a priest says solemnly but reflectively, like he's been beamed to the bedside while hearing a troubling confession and ponders the penance. He averts his eyes from Adele, as if hailed by someone in the room, and speaks more confidently. "You're in the Lord's hands now," he intones, looking directly at her. But he doesn't seem to see her. He mumbles what seems like a mixture of Latin and English.

Adele tries to make eye contact and join the sights and sounds. But it's like there's a filmy partition between them. And she can't figure what he's doing with his hands. He has a young face but it frightens her and gives the impression of being much older. The eyes are large leaden saucers that seem to have invaded most of the off-white border. She recoils from him as the fuzzy forms return. She feels like she's suspended in a vat of warm syrup.

Something brings her back. She sits up abruptly, clearheaded, as if exiting a dream to a carnival of peering faces. The priest, an elderly man in suit and hat, a slightly younger one with horn-rimmed spectacles who's clutching a bag, two middle-aged women wearing white uniforms, two other women wearing black, and Evelyn. She pans the group and

John O'Kane
San Pedro, CA

turns to each face, looking for something. The gazes continue. She falls back flat on the bed, no match for their power, feeling the touch of hands as everything goes blurry again.

"Adele!...we're here for you," Evelyn manages as Adele goes under. "He's ready to give you new life. Speak to him. Now's your chance!"

Adele swoons, opens her eyes to the elderly man who's clutching a stack of papers and gesturing to a male on her left who wears a stern expression.

"There's plenty of time for that," the doctor intercedes from her right, barely missing a beat.

The two women in black, peas in a pod, stand side-by-side in the corner away from the group, faces down, murmuring a patois of otherworldly. Rosary-ready ringers referred by a good Samaritan in the neighborhood, they seem oblivious to Adele. They finger their beads like guitarists searching for the lost chord and awaiting the end of the world as they know it.

Adele's eyes close to a rush of paralyzing pain and sounds she thinks come from above. They reopen to prison bars superimposed on the scene with the head of a male in his thirties staring out between them. The elderly man stands next to Adele and observes him. He then stares at her. She meets his eyes for an embarrassing instant and turns to the male who now vanishes. She closes her eyes again and reopens them to the elderly man who's taken his place. The bars dissolve and the scene rearranges. She sees heads huddled together in conversation. The priest turns from the group and observes her like he's preparing to caress a newly polished monstrance on the altar. She loses consciousness.

Evelyn tiptoes from the room and continues on to the stairs and hesitates, listening for sounds above. She thinks she hears something and slowly mounts the steps. At the top she meets the fearful eyes of a scrawny frame in the bedroom doorway and shepherds him inside, spreading her arms to shield him from possible noise. "Have you said your

John O'Kane
San Pedro, CA

prayers?" she asks. "Your mommy wants you to be close to the Lord!"

"What if she changes her mind?" the elderly man says to the doctor, who's preoccupied. "We've already worked everything out...just a matter now of..."

"...they never do...always see the light when it comes to their families," retorts the doctor. "Relax, there's nothing to worry about."

"She'll have a chance to see if she makes it...this place would be a curse anyway," a nurse says while reaching for an instrument.

"Yes, and when he's released it'll be like nothing ever happened," the elderly man chimes in, looking her directly in the eyes before turning to the doctor who meets it with a grin.

Adele jerks, wincing with pain. She opens her eyes and looks around frantically, like she's lost her sight. The doctor backs away from her as one of the nurses reaches for the hypo. The priest, who's apparently been meditating, approaches the bed. One of the women in black lurches toward Adele, beads a-clacking, her deathly mien morphing into a saintly aura. The priest produces a crucifix from his satchel and proceeds to open a Bible as everyone else gathers around the bed. A peaceful glow bathes their faces. Evelyn appears in the door frame, stopping abruptly. Her leaden expression softens and passes through a series of enigmatic contortions to a cherubic gawk. She reaches for her Bible.

Adele appears lifeless, barely breathing. All eyes are riveted on her every flinch.

"This moment...if only she...do you think she'll come out of it?" Evelyn asks the doctor.

"I think she should but...I don't get why she won't respond."

"Has she stopped breathing?" the priest interjects with a puzzled look on his face, eyes glued to the Bible's pages.

"Yes, I think she's...her throat is rattling slightly...or maybe she's..."

John O'Kane
San Pedro, CA

"...no, no, she's coming around," interrupts a nurse. "You can see her eyes opening slightly."

"Maybe it's a reflex."

Evelyn looks at Adele, but sees no movement. She smiles, and sobs slightly before beaming with pleasure, assured she's on to a better place and no longer suffering. All eyes are now on Adele, except for the two women in black who riff away on their beaded instruments, staring at an imaginary space on the floor. A calm settles over the group, a collective feeling that all good will has been spent in a job well done.

Adele sees a series of glowing heads without facial features, blank twitching blurs on an artist's canvas. She stares, waiting for the details, feeling her strength returning slightly.

"We've done all we can," the priest says, bringing his hands over Adele's body just shy of a clasp, like he might not be so sure. While contemplating how to form his gestures, Adele opens her eyes and lunges upright through his hands all in one movement, like waking from a pleasant dream. But she's clear-headed and wants to say something. The priest backs away, giving her the stage, waiting for her to speak.

"Who are you?" she asks, falling back on the bed but remaining alert. The nurses take their cue and move toward Adele, ready to take her pulse. The doctor grimaces, reaches for the hypo and then hesitates, looking directly into Adele's eyes with a puzzled expression. It gets very quiet as everyone holds their breath in anticipation. She lunges up again, forcing everyone away from the bed, looking from left to right at the arc of faces around her and back, fixing on Evelyn who immediately looks at the priest. She turns back to Adele but her funereal demeanor deflates and is no match for Adele's gaze. Evelyn turns away, fumbles with her Bible, then back to Adele.

"Well, what is it you want from me?" Adele says clearly to the group, like she's snapped out of a trance. She reaches out and touches the Bible, and smiles confidently before dis-

John O'Kane
San Pedro, CA

engaging from Evelyn who baby steps away from the bed.

"You feel you can just come in here and...what should I do now?"

No one speaks. The doctor turns to one of the nurses, and back to Adele who's gazing up at the ceiling, now oblivious to all in the room, like she's miming a private conversation with someone above. The priest fidgets, glances at the doctor and then Adele, who hasn't moved. She drops her head while keeping her poise and turns to the priest who looks at her suspiciously. Adele laughs uncontrollably.

"Well, what is it? I've listened to you...here I am. What's wrong?"

The two women in black, who've ceased fingering their beads, look up at Adele and appear bewildered. They jerk their frames to the left simultaneously, like Siamese twins, and exit the room with heads drooped.

"Just stay calm, my child...we'll...don't worry...I mean we'll make sure that you won't need.....anything," the priest finally manages as he stares into the eyes of one of the nurses.

Adele stares at him, perplexed, hoping he'll continue, say something that makes sense. She winces with pain but quickly recovers her composure and resumes staring. They back away, like they've seen a ghost, and return the stare. The doctor is virtually impaled against the dresser and appears mesmerized by something. Evelyn, who's been nervously teetering back and forth in the doorway, rushes Adele.

"Calm down...calm down!" blurts Evelyn, breaking the ice and smothering Adele with hugs. "What's wrong with you?"

Adele begins choking from the pressure, pushing Evelyn away with her remaining strength, finally succeeding. Evelyn backs off and retreats to the doorway with a whitening pallor. Adele appears stymied but recovers her relaxed confidence and smiles at them. Her smile seems to leave her lips with the power to freeze their gestures behind an imaginary glass barrier. A long silence follows.

John O'Kane
San Pedro, CA

A nurse twitches, turns to the group for a sign, and the barrier seems to disappear. She pulls a hypo from her bag like it's a Saturday night special, pivots to the priest's eyes and lurches toward Adele in one confident motion. Before Adele can resist she punctures her flesh, leaving her dazed.

Adele's smile becomes momentary caricature and then a soft frown before vanishing completely in a stuttering squeak. Her energy succumbs to the dispersing chemicals, but her eyes remain open. The nurse recoils from Adele's look, turning to the others whose vacant expressions offer no reassurance. The nurse checks her pulse and meets their eyes in apparent bewilderment, turning around to close Adele's eyes. Their facial gestures echo a shared sigh of relief.

Adele falls back toward the pillow in slow motion, nearly stopping every few inches like she's summoning the strength to reverse course, until her energy completely dissipates. She continues to look, seeing fuzzy shapes that change into something like a fading sunset of purplish smudges, and then a rush of heat followed by bright lights. It's so hot she can smell the heat. She's in a spacious room steaming with incense that gets larger and larger, making her feel as if she's disappearing. The heat lifts and the steamy odor evaporates, leaving her in a cool darkness.

***

Adele lies flat on the bed in the same position as when her eyes closed. There's no one in the room. Her face is bleached of pigment, giving the impression she's wearing a mask. But her lips are curled slightly upward, suggesting a transition toward either forming or deforming a smile. Barely audible voices can be heard from another room. They cease suddenly, as if she's been given a moment of silence for spirits to caress her. The stillness compounds. She seems to move slightly. The voices return and she opens her eyes, staring up at the ceiling.

John O'Kane
San Pedro, CA

Pain surges through her body like it's been given an electric charge. She lifts her arms and grasps her mid-section, wishing so bad for it to go away. The pain decreases and she raises her upper torso slightly, looks around the room and appears to recognize the surroundings. She inches her frame further upward, seeing her world displayed in a crescendo of rapture as if for the first time, meeting the metallic orbs on the wall. This gives her the strength to sit up level with the room. She notices the door is slightly ajar and feels drawn to it, easing her legs to the floor while trying to decipher the voices beyond.

Her baby steps get bigger as she reaches the door and peeks through the slit, bracing herself against the wall. She opens it wider and shuffles through, moving in rhythm to the shield of conversation, stopping with pauses. There's a swaddle of sheets and discolored blankets on the corner of a table that could be a load of wash someone left. It's graced by a few files and a scatter of papers that Adele peruses out of the corner of her eye as she leans against the table briefly, peering over the lip of the bundle like she's on the cusp of a bottomless cavern.

She cringes at the sight of the pale-pink prunish face. A warm numbness spreads through her body that pacifies the jolts of pain but leaves her vision blurred. It seems familiar but the nose is too large and it's like the bone structure and skin haven't fully fused. She wants to touch it, open its eyes and fast forward it, or pump it up with air as if it were an inflatable doll. Her vision settles momentarily and she thinks she sees herself, then perhaps a distant ancestor dozing in some cave. The voices cease briefly and return, breaking her concentration. All she can think of now is wrapping her arms around it, pulling it back toward its origins. She takes a few deep breaths and shuffles through the room to the kitchen, and on to the back door, hoping she can keep her footing. Once she reaches the sidewalk along the house she stops, looks behind her, and listens for the voices inside as she

John O'Kane
San Pedro, CA

hobbles across the neighboring yard toward the noisy street. As the traffic slows she continues through the lanes and against the chorus of honks to the median, finding her place of rest between a bush and a short concrete pillar. She unwraps the bundle, places it upright on the pillar, and waits.

***

Elmae Passineau
Weston, WI

Hearing Voices

If you were in Anchorage
   or Ogdensburg
how did your voice reach me
     travel through those long black lines
     strung from pole to pole
     across the country
serendipitous perches for weary birds
outlooks for predators or prey

And now,
your voice pings about in space
   and lands in my ear
images, too—
     sound, movement, color
     on my various screens
And my computer talks to my printer,
     abracadabra, a page sputters forth

Forget Houdini—
           THIS is magic!

Mark Biehl
Hales Corners, WI

Beyond

Oh no!
You fail to fool me
As you have others.
Pulling woolen covers
Over unsuspecting minds
And whispering licentious limericks
Into unhearing ears.
No more will I waltz to your
Metallic din—
Your raucous ragtime—
Your outrageous discord.
No longer will I bend to your
Seductive, hidden heresy.

***

Whispers

The wind,
Gentle on my cheek,
Hair teased
Then gone without a promise
Or a whisper of hope.
Gone suddenly beyond me
With sad eyes—
Weathered fingers beckoning

Julia W. Ridge
Portland, ME

Little Chick's Rap
Blunt Force Injury to the Abdomen

Little Chick.
I've never met her. Never seen her face—
fair, forsaken, flower girl of four.

Alone.

Trapped between hands that squeeze.
Punch-bag princess,
slapped silly and shoved against a wall.

"That's it! the monster said. "That's all!"

Alone, she is,

when blisters bubble like disease.
Fingers pinch.
Knuckles punch, punch, punch,
'till skin rips,
'till blood drip, drip, drips.

She, alone,

feels when baby brain
collides with cranial bone;

She, alone,

feels when Monster
does the work Monster
believes, but only Monster
feels relief.

Julia W. Ridge
Portland, ME

Who claims
her little heart?

Who blamed
her?

Who tamed
her
like she made o' nothin' but plaster
beneath the bone?

But plaster
only crumbles,
turns to dust,
blows away like seed.

Hearts break.
Bones shatter.
Organs shut down.

And plaster
don't look nothin' like viscera
when they bleed.

 "That's it!" the monster said. "That's all!"

Princess—fair heart—
only four.
Little Chick—
Little Chick lives no more.

Earl E. Weigelt
Winslow, ME

The Lovely Gloom

When a fog rolls in and wraps wraith's arms
around the Head, the cliffs and heath;

When the flats' chill promise adorns the air aboard the
    living mist
and blends aromas fleetingly 'twixt apples, balsams, red
    rose hips;

When the hulking spruces spread their wings in haunting
    black relief
and rear above the leaden ledge to shadow waters deep;

When seagulls jeer and herons croak and geese and seals
    groan
and sea-bells sound and fog horns blow and blueberry
    barrens moan;

It sinks its teeth into a man; it grips him firm and sure
and attends his dreams both day and night—

such is Downeast's allure!

Lisa M. Kristoff
Boothbay Harbor, ME

The Time Express

Mother, daughter, and son. The three stood quietly together by the shoulder of the road. The roar of the school bus announced the first day of school. Naomi, who had been busy removing smudge marks from her new black patent leathers, automatically stood up straight, a crooked smile on her lips. She tapped out morse code on her lunch box. Each touch echoed in the air. Dylan rigidly positioned himself next to Fonda, holding on to her with one hand while plunging his free hand in and out of his coat pocket. *Having a change of heart, baby? It's hard to believe this is the same little boy who tugged on my nightgown every morning yelling, "How many days left now, Momma?" Yea, Dylan, you're a big boy now. Hope you don't end up wishing you were little again.* She looked at his lunch box, the Superman box he'd begged her for, for months. His eyes, then as now, were excited, but apprehensive, his four-foot body twitching sporadically.

The school bus pulled up in front of them. Without even the quickest of glances, Naomi boarded the bus. Dylan looked up at Fonda, his hand now a fist in hers. "Well, bye, Momma." *Please don't cry, Dylan. Please.* "Off you go..." Fonda's voice broke off and with her free arm extended, indicated to her son his place was now with the other children. Obediently he let go of her hand. As the bus moved doggedly down the road, she caught sight of a face pressed against the emergency door window neither smiling, nor frowning. She blew him a kiss of support.

The oak door closed behind her, separating her from life, catching some air in motion voiced in a vacuum-like sound. She turned and was transported to a time before the children; when it was just the two of them: Michael and Fonda. She could smell the white pine of the cabin they rented, the fire glowing and warm in the field stone fireplace, the sky-

Lisa M. Kristoff
Boothbay Harbor, ME

lights in the loft bedroom. Winter in paradise. With her eyes closed she drew in a deep breath that escaped as a longing sigh.

She opened her eyes . The chaos of the kitchen brought her back to reality. *Ugh! Suburbia after breakfast...Do they really eat any of this stuff? Or is it just some kind of perverse exercise? The toaster sat in the center—crumbs below it like scattered leaves—a lone piece of wheat bread, half-toasted, remained—like the captain going down with the ship...Captain Fonda Wyatt reporting for duty, sir! After saluting the toast she observed pats of butter smeared into abstract designs, that created the illusion of a tablecloth—like illusions of marriage...Michael, why aren't you here anymore? ...Scrambled eggs floated in silenced snap, crackle, and pop—deaf ears ... Two half-full milk glasses were overturned as were the juice glasses—a dream-sicle river. I'd like to be a boat on that river...too late...that 'I do' blocked my passage...Instead I have one avant garde butter artist, a shy superhero and a missing husband....they do say it's lonely at the top.*

Fonda grouped her dishes in the sink. Mmm, boy! Nothing like slimy scrambled egg to give a morning that big finish...She reached under the sink and groped in the cupboard for a Handi Wipe. Crouching in front of the cabinet she stared at the package. *Always around for those 101 uses....Michael used to be...and some interesting uses indeed.*

Squirting the Joy dishwashing liquid in the water made the soap suds come alive in cartoon colors. *Soap suds and cocoa...Disney color...reliable color....Class! Class! Let's have your attention...this is a prism...magic glass...several dimensions...of itself...of life. Yes, Mrs. Reynolds. Like this washcloth falling into Technicolor suds; dispersing clouds turning in to Lawrence Welk bubbles ... A-one ... A-two ... Joy. An idiotic, but pleasing ironic name for a detergent. Sick humor for a lousy job....Proctor and Gamble's humor in uniform...Mary Hartman had a uniform...braids and pinafores...high old times for suburbanites only.*

Lisa M. Kristoff
Boothbay Harbor, ME

She raised the only surviving frying pan of Mom's hand-me-downs and stared into it. Moms and joy...bundles of joy...joy in the morning...to the world....Amen. In it Fonda inspected her reflection. A reflection that within seconds changed into the face of a young bride. Frustrated. Crying. Cinnamon stick hair...a black bandana...punk Cinderella...bridal joy...flash is out—eyes are in—the pan...brown-eyed frying pan woman.... Pan Airlines...having a wonderful time, wish you...She began to puncture the pan's bottom with a knife. Fonda dropped her mother's pan; let it slip in to the sea of joy.

She walked, ever so slightly off-balance, to face the mirror in the kitchen. Her hands traced her face and hair. She breathed deeply, closing her eyes. Steadiness regained, she returned to the sink. Grope in Joy for mother's pan...wash the mutilated, confessing pan...pull the drain plug and place the pan in the dish drainer...*Ooops! Pan goes in the can... Comprende? Ci. Ci. See. I've seen enough, thank you very much. Why all this nostalgia?...Why now...why at all? Get hold of yourself...Relax and have some tea...for moments like these...Thank you, Ms. Lawrence....*

Fonda filled the kettle and placed it on the stove. Turning it on to the high setting, she plucked her favorite red poppy tea cup from the dish drainer and began rummaging through the cabinet above that housed the tea tins. The bright packaging cheered her. Jasmine. Chamomile. Raspberry. Ginger. Selecting the pure white chamomile tin she watched it slip through her fingers and back in place on the shelf. *Empty? And still on the shelf? Imagine...*She grabbed the Jasmine tin, and, closing the cabinet door, spied Michael's coffee, and made a snarly face. Exclusively his—like time. Nicotine. Now that was another story. Her story. She found the smoke comforting. *Freud would say I'm fixed in the oral stage...appears he had a few fixations of his own...didn't you Mr. Freud?... "We all do, Fonda. Let's take you, for example...."* her conjured up Freud folds his hands on the kitchen table and con-

Lisa M. Kristoff
Boothbay Harbor, ME

tinues, "I believe you are repressing something. Prepare for anxiety, my dear..." *Goodbye Sigmund. I hate to cut you off...*Freud evaporates—except for his mouth, which lingers in front of her..."anxiety. Repression..." Fonda grinned. Imagine that, Freud looming like the Cheshire Cat.

Fonda removed a cigarette from the pack on the counter, sat back down, lit it, inhaled deeply and softly blew the smoke at the Freud lips, contentedly watching them dissipate. The piercing whistle of the kettle unnerved her. She jerked it off the burner and poured water and the tea bag in her cup. Drawing on her cigarette she began studying the wallpaper. Heart-bellied roosters and gold teakettles. *Red, gold, white, and green...popular back in the 40's...Today...ugh!* There was a time it appealed to her fondness for all things retro. Now...now, it represented something that had died a long time ago...*Hmm, maybe I should hotfoot it down to the home decorating place tomorrow...Need a project anyway...make some changes...*

Fonda finished her tea and smoke and walked down the short hall to the living room. *I wonder why they call it a living room? Is it because TV's and radios are always there? Turn on the radio—start living. Room.*

Fonda sighed, turned on the radio and sank into her favorite over-stuffed chair.

Her eyes fell on her wedding picture. Two radiant faces met hers. *Who are those people? ...look happy...why not...hear the man has a promising future as a copy writer with an up-and-coming ad agency...the woman?...she has two years of college...sure, she fancies herself a writer of sorts as well...Yep, she knows where she's headed....*

Next to their photo was an 8 X 10 of Naomi and Tory...*my future...like a failed ad campaign...*Fonda sank further in to the chair, now drawn into the haunting "Nocturnes." Her eyes closed. *If only it were possible to live in music like Mary Poppins and Burt romped through paintings.*

Unconsciously her hand dropped from the arm of the

Lisa M. Kristoff
Boothbay Harbor, ME

chair to the mahogany side table; her wedding band knocking on its glass top. *Anybody home?* Fonda turned her head in the sound's direction and cracked an eye, slowly lifting her hand, and leaving a perfect silhouette. *Like the kid's Kindergarten art...you'd never know I was raised by a woman who had a reputation for having the most immaculate house in the neighborhood.*

"You-hoo....feather duster..." Fonda sang in her best Jeanette MacDonald imitation, *When I'm calling you-hoo-hoo-hoo, hoo-hoo-hooo....* She walked to the livingroom closet for the feather duster. Lifting it up, Fonda shuddered...*Quick! Close the door. Don't want the skeletons to get out...*She slammed the door, headed for the table. Holding the duster at arms length above it she swung it slowly down in a pendulum-like movement. Slowly bringing it closer, closer to the offending print. Then, with quick determined strokes the dust particles fell through the air downward. *Thanks for the memory, Edgar. Yes, Mrs. Shaw?...'Miss Wilson, I think you've had enough exposure to Poe; sober up with Dickinson!...' Humph. Still life sure is sobering.*

The duster glided over the rest of the furniture. Hmm, Fonda mused, only the cocktail dress is missing...When she reached the bookcase, her eyes surveyed each title. *Anna Karenina, The Fountainhead, Love Poems of Ovid, Alice in Wonderland, A Room of One's Own.* She looked quickly away. Her eyes burned with tears.

She touched the bindings and was transported back to college...*Miss Wilson, you've got talent. Develop it and use it wisely...Finish your education!....* Voices of professors flooded through the dam of her memory. *Here live the dreams of Fonda Wilson Wyatt.* She raised the duster over her head, just as the grandfather clock bellowed the time.

She sank to the floor, facing her treasures, one leg down, one leg bent at the knee—a prop for her auburn head. A Simon and Garfunkel passage buzzed through her head, "...Time, time, time, look what's become of me..." Then the

Lisa M. Kristoff
Boothbay Harbor, ME

Chambers Brothers, "... Now the time has come, there are things to realize....time has come today..." Time has come to Day...*I've been like the textbooks, like an old train out of steam. Ladies and Gents, we are now pulling out of Repression Station, please have your tickets ready...All aboard the Time Express....*

Fonda cried softly until the squealing brakes of the school bus quieted her. *Time has come for me...time to remember forgotten dreams.* She wiped away her tears with fingertips, then drew herself up.

"Mom! Mom!" The children's shrill voices and laughter carried into the living room. Fonda knelt down as Naomi held up her latest art work in her face. *Looks like we scraped up a layer of breakfast tablecloth*, she thought while saying, "It looks great, pumpkin!" Fonda hugged Naomi and saw Dylan standing close behind his sister. He moved to the left, and sheepishly offered his accomplishment of the day—a hand silhouette.

Hugging Dylan, Fonda flashed them a big smile and asked, "How're my candy-apple faces after their long, hard day?" Naomi joined her brother in her mother's arms. Naomi managed to wriggle out of her mother's embrace and caught a tear on her finger. With arched eyebrows she surveyed Fonda's face.

"And how was your day, Mama?" Her tone surprised Fonda.

"I don't know about you two, but I'm starving," Fonda said changing the subject, "Ready for snacks?"

The children exchanged glances, shrugged and continued appraising their mother.

"Mom, are you hungry?"

"Famished, Naomi."

"Wh-what does that m-mean," asked Dylan with a quizzical expression, while moving in closer to his sister who seemed to be handling things.

Fonda grinned, "It means Mama's fast is over."

Patricia Janke
Wauwatosa, WI

Specks, Flecks and Other Muses

Time travels besides floating
specks of molecules dusting
Earth's landscape;
I contemplate tiny silent beats
second after second unfolding
Human fate;
Strings vibrate through space
building blocks of our universe
Time forever in motion;
that second never to be relived-
conditioned emotion rises and
falls with tides of the ocean;
Spirit drifts alongside existing
In this framed mirror of life;
A low hum pulsates through
Each fleck heard in three-fourth's
time dancing in the universe

***

Sally Belenardo
Branford, CT

Blind

You know the saying long renowned:
A picture's worth a thousand words.

To those who see the world through sound,
a song is worth a thousand birds.

Irene Zimmerman
Greenfield, WI

This Morning

when the sun vaulted
above the trees shouting
It's a great day to be alive!

I found a baby robin lying
on wet grass
with naked, broken wing—

a tiny, pitiful thing
fallen from its nest
in the unreachable sky

never, never to sing.

***

Between Seasons

Something's falling—rain or snow—
outside
on trees that have no place to go
to hide.
Half-naked, caught between the seasons,
they stand tall.
I search unquietly for reasons
for it all
and learn from them at last to stand
in tears and tatters.

God's making each of us by hand.
That's all that matters.

MJ Herrling
Bradley, ME

Brother Dave

Well, now, they often call me Speedo,
but my real name is Mr. Earl.

—Ry Cooder

I was too young then,
you said,
but I found a fender, smooth
and violet-hued, perfect
for your '40 Ford.
Stinking junkyard men consumed
every word about Craig and you
passing a green sedan full
of drunken girls doing
a hundred and ten
down Mystic Hill. Later
Craig turned 24, but he passed 70
the night he flew
in his gray Chevrolet.
When you hauled home his 45s,
the mahogany cabinet
was his crew cut,
the green cases,
his eyes. We rode
in your black Ford to see the elm
where Craig's laugh
hung still.

P. C. Moorehead
North Lake, WI

Blooming

Blooming roses,
growing indiscriminately,
covering the snow—
a blanket of grace.

Blanketing myself,
wrapping me,
sheltering me
from the cold.

Warming me,
heating me,
thorning me,
that I might grow.

***

Far Star

I am a far star,
glimmering faintly,
shining in the night.

Look at me.
Telescope me.
Catch my light.

Move beyond.
See!
My light shines brighter.

Peggy Faye Brown
Gray, ME

Bangor Public Library

Doors of light oak, masterfully carved and enormous like those of a castle entrance, welcome me atop the granite steps. In childhood, those steps could not be conquered without my patient father holding my hand and helping me reach the top. Brass handles did not require great strength as the doors opened easily, smoothly, presenting a grand entrance with doorways large enough for a full and fancy dress of the 1800's to pass through. How many of my ancestors also passed through these same doors?

Visits to the Bangor Public Library are one of my favorite childhood memories. As a little girl, I felt like I was visiting a castle and it was mine to explore. Hours were spent on each visit exploring the books in the children's room and finding a cozy spot to disappear on a literary adventure. I look through the large wooden doorway to the room where my pasture of childhood adventures took place but it has changed; table, computers and adults now fill the room. Sigh, things change over time. Fanciful memories remain in my mind as the world cannot remain the same. As I explore other areas of the building, however, I discover that great expansion has happened and many wonderful spaces have been created for the new generations to explore and learn.

We did not have wealth in my family, but we had curiosity which we knew led to wisdom. My parents gave me a wonderful gift by taking me to the library frequently which inspired a lifelong joy; the love of reading, writing, family history and the appreciation of libraries. All for free. I could dream of being a farmer girl with her own horse, or a scientist, a writer, a traveler, an astronaut, or a dreamer all in the safe surroundings only five miles from home with my protective parents in the building.

The twin curved stairways of beautiful, wide marble steps

Peggy Faye Brown
Gray, ME

invite me upstairs. All these years later, they still fill me with awe. At the top is a gorgeous circular chandeliered rotunda with the names of literary giants commemorated all around. I get dizzy looking up in adoration and soaking in their names, some unknown to me, but others produce a vision in my adult mind of a snippet of their work. Longfellow, Hawthorne, Emerson. All is quiet in this library castle but I sense whispers of greatness surrounding me.

The lovely curved handrail glides me back downstairs. Descending the wide, smooth marble steps, I turn to catch one last glimpse of the rotunda: exquisite. At the foot of the stairs I enter another large doorway and discover wooden card catalogs along an inner wall of the local history room. An affinity for card catalogs swells in my nostalgic soul as other library admirers can understand and appreciate. Searching the web does not provide the gratifying exploration, at least for me, as flipping the index cards to discover a title, topic or author.

I discover that the genealogy section has been moved downstairs to this room. I open the C drawer, that of my maiden name. I find names of my ancestors on the index cards which list newspaper archives over several decades. My dad has three index cards: his poem published in WWII, the newspaper article announcing his invention patent, and lastly, his obituary. Sigh, things change over time.

Lilli Buck
Bristol, VA

The Road to Stalingrad

When first we came to Russia,
We were singing as we went,
Expecting some great victory,
Some historical event.

We sang "Deutschland Uber Alles,"
And "Die Fahne Hoch,'
And German beer hall drinking songs,
Until the heavens spoke.

It was then we saw a big black cloud
Spread all across the sky.
"Go back, go back, you German soldiers.
Go back or you will die."

But we could not go backwards.
We had orders to obey,
Though we should sacrifice our lives,
And perish in the fray.

So like lambs led to the slaughter,
Or like lemmings that rush to the sea,
We marched deeper into Russia,
The Sixth Army of Germany.

Then we heard the weird ghosts whisper
Ghosts from long ago.
"Go back, go back, you German soldiers,
Or you will perish in the snow."

Lilli Buck
Bristol, VA

"No, do not go to Stalingrad.
Go back another way.
Go back, go back to Germany,
And live another day."

I dreamed I saw a grenadier
In Napoleonic uniform,
Huddling around a fire,
Trying to keep warm.

"Go back, you German soldier.
Go back while there is time,
Or you will die like we did,
And leave your bones behind.

"Go back, you German soldier.
Your mission it must fail,
For Russia will destroy you,
With snow and ice and hail."

Then the soldier fell to a skeleton
Who was living a while ago.
Then his bones fell to the earth,
And were buried in the snow.

We feared not the Russian winter.
It was six months away,
For we left at height of summer,
Upon a sunny day.

So we headed across the plain,
To capture Stalingrad.
We didn't know at that time yet
How things would get so bad.

Lilli Buck
Bristol, VA

We heard the wild wolves howling
At the frozen moon,
And with the whipping wind,
It made an eerie tune.

We heard the lost souls wailing
In a not-too-distant Hell,
Still weeping for their lives they lost,
When catastrophe befell.

Now we came to the River Don,
And the wind began to blow.
It was the start of winter,
And it began to snow.

But we made it into Stalingrad,
And captured it in part.
We raised the Swastika overhead,
Which brought joy to our hearts.

And to the Slavs of Russia
We did anything we liked,
To rob them and to shoot them,
For the glory of the Reich.

But when Von Paulus took over,
He stopped our war crimes,
That we might treat our enemies
With decency all the time.

We dug trenches outside the city,
In the ice and in the snow.
The weather it grew colder,
Down to thirty degrees below.

Lilli Buck
Bristol, VA

We ran out of food and ammo.
We ran out of gasoline,
And what little gas we had left at all
Froze up in our machines.

With frostbite in our fingers
And frostbite in our toes,
We had no winter clothing,
And it was 35 below.

We had no strength left
With which to stand and make a fight,
So we just waited to be shot,
Just like a deer out in the night.

The Red Army surrounded us
Until there was no hope.
Then they took us prisoner
When we could no longer cope.

When the Russians took us prisoner,
We had not eaten for four days,
So we hoped that they would feed us
When they hauled us all away.

But we had to march a hundred miles
To a Russian prison camp,
Where they just starved us further
In the clammy, cold, and damp.

Farewell, farewell to Germany
Whom we'll never see again.
Farewell, farewell to an army
Of 300,000 men.

Lilli Buck
Bristol, VA

I guess we got our karma
For it comes back again,
And the Russian Army did to us
Just what we did to them.

***

Peggy Trojan
Brule, WI

All That Matters

In her nineties
my mother's memory
got stuck on the present.
"Where did Pa go?"
she would ask sweetly,
I could tell her
but minutes later
she asked again.

Once I tried to get her
to recall Paris when Jerry
was doing graduate work.
She couldn't remember.
Finally she asked,
"Did I have a good time?"
"Yes! You and Dad
had a wonderful trip!"
"Well," she said,
looking me in the eye,
"that's all that matters."

Thomas Peter Bennett
Silver Spring, MD

Aquarian Celebration

Wow! Wow!
Two in a row. . .
A meteor shower
radiating from Aquarius.

Earthly visible in
Nature's planetarium,
framed by treetops,
above a darkening pond.

The Aquarids were
brief flaming illuminations,
balls of fire in the sky . . .
giant, frosted raindrops at night
from Aquarius.

They excited a barred owl,
frogs' chorus, water bugs,
slugs and me. . .

In our Aquarian celebration
around the ebony pond, in
the marshy aromatic forest.

Fred Cheney
Bowdoinham, ME

Biscuit Barnes: Hired Pen

For someone who had a history of being a dumpy little guy, he was looking pretty buff that day striding across the fairgrounds of Pelham Junction. Rather than a baseball hat, worn sideways as was the fashion of his peers, he had a green visor pulled low and aimed straight ahead. He wore a powder blue vest, a bow tie, white shirt, and suspenders that had the color and striping of garter snakes. Chino pants and beige and brown saddle shoes completed the picture. However, no amount of looking good would allow him to out-grow his nickname for nearly twelve years: Biscuit.

He painted a somewhat comical picture struggling along trying to keep hold of a rickety old card table and a fake alli-gator-skin suitcase. The card table was the old kind made of cardboard, and eventually warped from liquids spilled and hot casserole dishes left on it too long. Under his other arm, the suitcase was about double the size of a laptop bag and held together with duct tape and dirty clothes line.

Biscuit was a familiar sight. In addition to the county's agricultural exposition, he had appeared at the town's Fourth of July barbecue, Old Home Days, and the various festivals of the neighboring towns—the Seafood Festival, the Egg festival, and the Antique Car Rally. He'd been a fixture since his freshman year in high school, and now his senior year was about to get under way.

"Hey, Dud-leeeee, good to see ya, you handsome dog," yelled Mavis from the fried dough concession. Mavis knew that everyone called him Biscuit, but he was Dudley to her.

Biscuit stopped to visit. "Hi, Mavis. How's it been out there on the road." He liked Mavis and her husband, Woody. They lived in a van outfitted with a bed, a TV, and a microwave. They towed a trailer that opened up into a food stand, if fried dough can be considered food. Their conces-

Fred Cheney
Bowdoinham, ME

sion, called "Torte Reform—Funnel Cakes and Fried Dough," was Woody's sense of humor, pure and simple.

"I don't know, Dudley. Sometimes I think I'm too old to travel with this old carnival any more. Up and down. Up and down. Michigan, Ohio, Iowa. Sleep and drive. Sleep and drive. But, you know, Woody and me, we don't know any different. Hey, you're looking good. Have you grown taller, or lost some weight."

"Both, I guess. I went out for cross-country last year just to see if I could slim down. I was awful at it, but I acquired some better habits. And I guess I did lose a little weight along the way."

"Some. You look really good. I suppose that means I can't swap one of your masterpieces for some fried dough."

"No offense, Mavis. I am off stuff like fried dough, but we don't have to swap. Just come by when you have time. I'll fix you right up because you're my favorite. Got to go now, but come see me."

Biscuit made his way down the row of booths—ring toss, dunk-a-dope—and exhibits—spinning wool, wood carving with chain saws, and leather crafts. Eventually, he found the spot that he had rented, a half-sized opening between Walter Snipe, the guitar and fiddle repairman, and Elsa Connover, the palm reader.

Elsa waved to him. "Bert Cousins brought by three folding chairs for you, and left 'em with me, so you don't have to go over to the dining tent."

"Thanks for lookin' out for me, Elsa. Hey Walter. I'll bet that fiddle of yours has got a song trapped inside that's just busting to get out."

Walter looked up from adjusting a string and grinned. "You might be right, Biscuit." And with that he brought the fiddle up underneath his chin and liberated "Saint Anne's Reel."

Biscuit laughed and quoted a line from "The Mountain Whip-poor-will," that he knew Walter was fond of. "Never had

Fred Cheney
Bowdoinham, ME

a brother ner a whole pair of pants, But when I starts to fiddle, why, yuh got to start to dance!" He made a clumsy attempt at a clog dance, and Walter's song dissolved into laughter.

But now it was time to get down to business. Biscuit unfolded the legs of the card table and adjusted it on the lumpy ground. One leg had a mind of its own and protruded way off to one side, but that was part of the charm. He put the two folding chairs on one side and the other directly across from them. Then he bent over and untied the clothes line holding the suitcase shut. First out was a tattered manila envelope with a few dozen sheets of paper in it. The canvas money pouch stayed inside.

And then, the star of the show. A genuine, two-tone— aquamarine and cobalt blue—Ollivetti portable typewriter. As small and light as it was, it still nearly collapsed the decrepit card table. For the final touch Biscuit took some duct tape and affixed a hand lettered sign saying, "The Poet is In."

While, Biscuit, as he himself said, stunk up the cross-country course, he did know what he was doing when it came to words. People would sit down, look at this fresh-faced kid dressed like an old time newspaper reporter, and it usually would go like this.

Customer: "So you write poems for people?"
Biscuit: "Yes, I do."
C: "If you write one for me, will it rhyme and everything?"
B: "If you want it to rhyme, it'll do that."
C: "So what will you write about?"
B: "It's your poem. It's about whatever you want it to be about."
C: "Do you keep a copy? Like to publish later?"
B: "Nope, you get the only copy. I don't even put my name on it."
C: "Can I put my name on it? Like I wrote it?"

Fred Cheney
Bowdoinham, ME

> B: "You can, but I charge a lot more if you're going to do that."
> C: "So, what is your basic charge?"
> B: "Twenty-five cents a line. Most of them go about 16 lines."
> C: "But, if somebody wants more...?"
> B: "I'm working for you. One guy, one time, he wanted a whole epic ballad of his softball team's championship season. It was six or seven pages. Cost him around a hundred bucks."
> C: "Was it hard?"
> B: "There aren't a lot of rhymes for the word single. And he remembered every single, single."
> C: "Okay, I want a poem. What do I have to do?"
> B: "First tell me who you want the poem for."
> C: "It's my sister. She's in the Air Force."
> B: "Now tell me about her. What makes her special? What makes her poem special?"

Biscuit would sit and listen. He took no notes. He didn't touch the typewriter or a piece of paper. He didn't have a stock list of questions, or things that should be covered. He just let folks talk until they ran out. Then he would scroll a piece of paper into the carriage of the typewriter. Often at this point, he would ask the customer if he could just review one little incident. Biscuit didn't do this because he hadn't been paying attention. He did it because he wanted to hear how the customer edited it the second time through. What got left out, what got amplified.

He would then tap out the first four lines or so, and turn the typewriter around for the customer to read. "Does this seem to have the kind of feel you want?" Usually Biscuit had it right, but if not, he'd scroll another sheet of paper in the machine and take a different approach.

Today had been a good day, often with people actually waiting in line. Phillip Landry, for his business partner's

Fred Cheney
Bowdoinham, ME

retirement. The Sanderson twins, for their mother. Mayor Sugg, for his granddaughter in Fairbanks, Alaska. Darla Breem, for Chip, the quarterback.

The lights on the midway were all up, and some evening dew was starting to make things sticky and moist. Biscuit decided that before he left, he'd tap out something for Mavis and Woody. She hadn't gotten over for that visit, but he'd sort of had her in the back of his mind much of the day. He scrolled a piece of paper into the carriage.

He lost track of how long he had been staring at the empty sheet, but suddenly a slight movement caught his eye. Carly Fitzsimmons was sitting across the table from him.

He caught his breath. Carly was beautiful. There was no other way to say it. Her hair was perfect, like silk. It caught the colors of the sun and improved them, and tonight it was doing the same for the midway lights—the rides, the booths, the tents. Her complexion was pure, deep, and hypnotic. There was something regal about the way she carried herself, yet she wasn't snobby at all. She often smiled at Biscuit when she was getting things from her locker in the hallway at school. The other day, she'd even asked him if he was running cross-country again. Breathless, he could only nod that he was. The word man, speechless. She went on to say that she admired how anyone could run for three miles. She knew she couldn't.

Biscuit knew Carly's schedule, particularly when she would be using her locker, which was two down from his. He made a point of doing his locker business at the same time she went to hers. He told himself it wasn't like stalking, just making the most of his day.

Biscuit tried to shake off the confusion her looking at him was causing, and hoped he wasn't going to have to write a poem about one of the football goons who stuck his head in the toilet that time. Actually, he wasn't sure who Carly was going out with. She went out some, but never seemed to stay with anybody for any length of time.

Fred Cheney
Bowdoinham, ME

He tried to control his voice, get enough wind to push a few words out his mouth. "Hi, Carly. I didn't expect to see you here."

"Hi Dudley. You mean here at the fair? My parents have an exhibit, and I had to help. It's not all that strange, is it?"

Biscuit immediately started to babble. Of course, it wasn't unlikely that Carly would help out her parents. It was that she was at his table. Not that she wouldn't have some-one important in her life. His mind swirled. Carly smiled, reached across the table, and tapped the back of his hand. "I'm here for a poem, Dudley. Can we go to work?"

Biscuit jumped a bit, and tried to focus on the place her fingertips had landed, tried to keep the feeling from going away.

Biscuit: "Sure. Right. Ah, okay, who is the person?"
Carly: "That'll come later."
Biscuit: "Whatever you say. But you'll have to give me
        something to work with."
Carly: "Sure. The poem is for a guy."
Biscuit: "And he's definitely 'poem-worthy'?"
Carly: "Poem-worthy is a really good way to put it."

Biscuit settled into his usual listening disposition, wait-ing for information, and listening to the tones, particularly the tones, as the information flowed. He forgot it was Carly—Carly Fitzsimmons—sitting over there providing the ore that would be refined into a poem. He got past the magical tones and rhythms that came so naturally to her, and he started absorbing the information about the poem-worthy guy in Carly's life.

Carly went on carefully and methodically about the sub-ject of her poem, but Biscuit noticed that she was more vague than most people in giving the details. There was a lot of feeling and affection, but nothing about a first date, or a skating party, or canoeing, or a favorite song; those were the

Fred Cheney
Bowdoinham, ME

places most people went first. The person was definitely special but in a weirdly distant sort of way. Biscuit, while acknowledging a slight personal loss, felt good for this somebody Carly felt so good about. He was also looking forward to the challenge of getting this amorphous sort of narrative into a poem. He wasn't sure how he would do it, but that was the fun. That was why he put himself out here at the fairs and the old home days. But she was going to have to give him something concrete to anchor the whole thing. He kept listening. And listening.

And then he was aware, that she was done. She'd stopped telling about the guy, and she was looking at him, leaning forward a bit. Smiling, looking at him. Leaning forward a bit.

Biscuit caught his breath and realized he didn't have enough to ask for more details about one salient little part. He hadn't really heard anything salient, just a lot of softness. If only this guy had hit a single in softball, just one single time.

"Ah, . . . Okay Carly. Is there . . . anything else you can think of?" He was dead in the water, and he knew it.

"Yeah. I've got one absolute requirement. I want the title to be one word, and I want it to rhyme with "flood free.""

Carl Little
Mount Desert, ME

The Rabbit Fire
For Amy Pollien

When father set the pile of old barn aflame
a rabbit came running out, its fur
setting fire to the landscape
as it raced past us gathered there

including a few firemen invited to the show
who leapt to douse flames
that fled into the distance before
further conflagration could take place.

We still refer to that night as "the rabbit fire"
and I, a young witness to the fiery sight,
wonder at what we've since witnessed
that far outshines the leaping creature sparking grass:

whole cities transformed into fire pits
and masses of families fleeing.
And yet that terrified animal and its burning trail
refuse to fade from the mind's eye

no matter how dark grow the skies
with smoke of burning buildings,
no matter how many women, men and children
perish on the road to some far-off freedom,

their eyes burning in the night.

Andrea Suarez-Hill
Jonesboro, ME

yearlings

grey bamboo bones
                blend
                    into last year's grass

ebony eyes
        meet man
           white flags fly

birch-paper skins
          unfurl
            flutter with March wind

they flee
      finch-light
        on lithe green shoots

fleet as arrows
        freed to the air
            both wear

flora-fauna symmetry

Maxine Seekins
Searsport, ME

The Christmas Memories

The memories they all seem so special to me,
The smell of the real pine tree,
The bubble lights,
The ornaments, shiny and bright,
The homemade skirt under the tree,
The simple presents placed for my siblings and me,
The angel at the top,
The smell of the pine needles that drop,
The popcorn and cranberry garlands were a must,
My grampa's big box of apples for us.
The love of the Christmases we shared,
The family filling every chair.
The smell of the kitchen at hand,
Chickens roasting in a pan,
The smell of stuffing,
The breakfast muffins,
And apple pie for you,
The pumpkin and mincemeat pies too,
Lemon pie with meringue piled high,
Don't forget the fruitcake,
I just couldn't wait!
What a workout my nose got,
With mashed potatoes in a pot.
Homemade pickles and more,
Gravy and boiled onions galore.
Peas and squash and cranberry sauce.
How grateful I was for each year,
This was part of my Christmas cheer.
There were nuts to crack and ribbon candy,
Homemade fudge placed so handy.
These memories make me smile, like a turn of a Christmas
        dial.

Maxine Seekins
Searsport, ME

As i think of the child born on Christmas Day
And all He stands for even today.
I think about the Christ Child's blessing
What a glorious lesson.
I thank God for Jesus' birth always.
I thank God for his love every day, as I pray.
I want to wish you a Merry Christmas and a Happy New
       Year!
May God bless you all!

***

Thomas Peter Bennett
Silver Spring, MD

Pond Darkness

After dark,
after the rain,
they gather pond side
and begin a grunting chorus.

They survey the
pond's expanse and
the miasma of fog
over its shimmering surface.

Some dive into the
dark unknown, searching
for water bugs and slugs.
Those onshore continue with
chorus croaking cheers.

Susan van Alsenoy
Wiscasset, ME

Pumpkin Farming

In the early spring I get down on my hands and knees
      and tuck each sleeping seed into the still cold soil;
      then I give it a pat, wish it good luck, and pray for
            some sun.
Within two weeks the land begins to live—
      pumpkin plants sprout from the graves of their
            seeds.
But they are not alone—other vegetation appears
      without invitation, intercession, or apparent origin.
The hitherto quiet, rustic countryside becomes a
      battlefield, forcing me to defend my chosen with a
      long-stemmed hoe, stained with streaks of green,
      against the heathen interlopers who have stinging
            nettles
      to snare the unwary.
The confrontation continues for many days until suddenly,
      without warning, the pumpkin plants explode their
      leaves, and victory is assured.
Come Fall the green leaves wither, revealing their bright,
      orange prize,
      and I know the battle was more than worth the
            while,
      as I enjoy excited children's happy Halloween smiles.

Sherry Ballou Hanson
Portland, OR

Hanging at the Car Show

I knew nothing when I arrived to exhibit my killer red, 1988 Pontiac Formula Firebird with the small V8 engine at the 14th annual Midcoast Auto Show in Bath, Maine, on August 24, 2008. Some facts were obvious pretty quickly: muscle cars predominated. Masters of the cars were mostly male; and yes, my fantasy car from the late 1950s—a block-long Chevy Impala convertible that puts today's Impala model in the category of "wus"—was in abundance.

I became aware of other aspects of the show as the morning passed. After I had been there for a couple of hours I noticed that the first arrivals in specific classes of cars—like muscle cars, best-of the 50s, Mustangs, etc.—were often the best in that category in the end, at least in my uninformed opinion. These were usually the most tricked-out entries. As I made my first walk-around I saw several cars with mirrors on the under side of their open hoods and tiny models of the cars sitting in there. Very cute. My opinion was not worth much in that department, as it turned out, when a screaming metallic neon green 1993 Mazda RX3 that should have got best-in-show, if there was such a class, shut down its hood and skulked off home with no award at all.

Most of the exhibitors seemed to know each other and probably voted for each other's chariots, as long as they were not competing in the same class. We all got one vote in each class of cars. The veterans brought sun canopies and coolers. This was good, as when August sun finally burned through the coastal fog that field turned into scorched earth and I mooched some shade behind one of The Bird's competitors, a hot red Camaro Z28 LT1 30th edition. I brought my reliable peanut butter and margarine sandwich and some fruit. Who knows what was in the coolers, but if you wanted something other than a burger and fries while baking out

Sherry Ballou Hanson
Portland, OR

there on the field, you had to bring your own. I am sure the sponsors—Bath Park & Rec and Knights of Columbus—prohibited alcoholic beverages on site. A cool beer would have slid down good out on the parched field while all the hard work of judging was going on.

I watched the people, mostly men like I already said, and there were quite a few '60s types like me. Many wore black T-shirts, cultivating the bad-ass image (what is it with black t-shirts in the sun anyway? Don't these people have sweat glands?) and sporting beer guts (unlike me; I favor the cut look myself) and they visited each other, talking cars and who knows what else. Few of these geezers paid any attention to me or The Bird. The young guys, like that Mazda owner, and the equally young lord of a totally custom, 1997 sapphire blue, metallic Dodge Neon with doors that opened upwards, were bursting to talk about their entries, even to "older" females like me. Adjacent to me in the Firebird/Camaro class was another red 1997 Firebird, and from the teenaged-owner I learned quite a few tips about tricking out our cars, though this was his first show too.

Understand The Bird is 20. She has had a paint job, so she looks killer, and her interior is all original. I've owned her for 17 years and both the first owner (female) and I took care of her. No beer bashes in the back seat (ya' can't fit back there anyway), so no puke stains, and no booneying in the cornfields of Illinois from whence I brought her in the spring of 1992. But there are no mirrors beneath the hood. I haven't been hanging out under there except to check fluids and snatch out dead leaves. After wintering over in the garage, I scope for dead rats and feral cats but never have found any. The owner of the 1997 Firebird next to my car told me to spray the engine with degreaser, hose her down, then use the foam formula of Armoral brand vinyl protectant on hoses and metal parts. I plan to do this, as it seems like a quick fix for 20 years on the road. I have replaced the gas shocks that hold up her rear deck three times and I learned there is a

Sherry Ballou Hanson
Portland, OR

heavier duty model of shocks that would better support my serious spoiler sitting on back. I'll look into that too, as the third set of shocks also died. While I am on the topic of gas shocks, those puppies under the hood that croaked last year can be replaced for $10 or less. I do know a wrench from a hair dryer, so maybe I could do it myself. The young guys were encouraging; I might give it a try while my enthusiasm lasts.

Other stuff like doors opening upwards and the adorable little model of the car sitting under the hood I will leave to the young fellows who are into this look. The car show was fun. Rock music from the '50s and '60s pumped, reminding me of my former life as a fine young thing back in the Stone Age, and the cars were awesome, really. Think about all that traveling history and adventure sitting there in that one field! There were several items raffled off and a 50/50 that gave the winner $147. I won nothing, but I got to vote in every category except mine. I scoped out all Chevelle SS rides because one of my sons is a serious gear head. I even spied a dark green AMC Javelin from the 1970s, another cool car in its day. I used to own a periwinkle blue model, one of the last made, but it went through two sons in addition to me and did not look so hot in the end. The whole deal was worth the $10 entry fee and I got a T-shirt. I hope The Bird got a thrill from the impressive company she kept that day.

At the awards ceremony a bunch of the car show veterans and assorted mavericks gathered their chairs and coolers and swiped most of the trophies. Like I said, they all appeared to know one another and had obviously been here and done this, many times. But it was rewarding to see a young kid in his first show bag a runner-up award. I heard a couple of older men talking and one said to the other that he "liked seeing these young guys with their own car clubs because the older clubs shunned them." Politics. It's everywhere. The Bird and I had a good time and we'll go again some day.

Jonathan Pessant
Durham, ME

the impermanence of being alone

forget-me-not

i invited my cousin and his girlfriend, both half my age,
to walk the craggy coastline beyond Winslow Park.
and as we climbed down the embankment, i was awash
with doubtless serenity as the late day sun rippled its
warmth and affection upon this moment in September.

we let our toes recede within the soft sand of the tide's
outgoing wake. living crabs remained still like the
dead ones, until prodded by the removal of a perfect
stone to skip upon the smooth face of the Atlantic.

after a while i asked him, "which do you prefer to live
next to, the forest (in which he grew up in), or the ocean?"
he laughed, his back slightly slanted, his arm winding up,
"the forest, but this isn't too bad either."

and i thought to myself, that if all would have gone
to plan, i might now have a son like him, or a daughter
like her. and still thinking, as they played at the future
and i at the knowing of my own receding tide,
that our lives are like that skipped stone.

marigold

my niece and i shared a joint close to the summit of
Bradbury Mountain. the past wants to be as lost
as the future. and as we reached the top, the
daytime moon greeted us with a welcoming wink.
we laughed. October is a good time for family and
to be high, in the clouds and in our minds.

Jonathan Pessant
Durham, ME

we sat upon a large glacial remnant, our legs hanging
over, our feet approving of the opposing gravity.
after a while she asked me what i dreamt about last
night (her crazy uncle always was remembering his
dreams. she took after me she said once.) a dream
journal in which we espoused the sublime sacred
laid upon her lap, pencil poised.

i often thought that my own daughter would have
been like her, unafraid and unabashed. and as i
recounted to her my dream of a daytime moon and a
wisp of laughing smoke and a mountain, i warned
myself that this life is like a leaf swaying in the
October breeze, and fall's breath upon my back
whispered the coming of death. the leaves blanketed
the earth, gentle red and sullen yellow, reminding
me that rebirth is still too far away.

chrysanthemum

i didn't know that yesterday was family day
at the art museum at Bowdoin College. many
running children and disinterested moms and dads,
a young attendant asked me to watch my children.
i simply remarked that i had no children.
"oh, i'm sorry," she offered. "no need to be," i smiled.

i am constantly reminded that i will be the only
male in my family that will not bear a child, an
heir, a junior, continuing a last name easily
forgotten eons from now, when the earth is swallowed.
i was married once, wasn't that good enough?

Jonathan Pessant
Durham, ME

sometimes i think i am a man between two
eras, two minds, two motivations, two
imaginations. sometimes i choose neither
of them, and wake crying. sometimes i choose
both, and come ever closer to realization.
sometimes i feel i am November,
and that my only children will be me.

***

Sylvia Little-Sweat
Wingate, NC

Elegy for my Father

The day we buried you
an autumn sky
could not have known.
It was so blue.

Along the stubble fields
sassafras fired
oaks, then grass,
a reddish hue.

Gold chrysanthemums
that banked your grave
were setting suns
on days—too few.

Despite October light
our hearts were shades
of winter days,
our loss—so new.

Sarah J. Woolf-Wade
New Harbor, ME

The Brook

For years, my own ancient stream
rippled its way among the thickets
from scratchy arms of uncut trees
to mossy fields of wild blueberries
out of shadows into sunshine
under brilliant August heat
winding down from hill to sea
a bubbling guide for my feet.

If ever I would wander, lost
in tangled stand of evergreens,
fluttering water would guide me on
through the pathless underbrush
of sunless virgin woods,
my ear trained toward the hum
of lobster boats not far away
at its ending, on the bay.

Now it slips through treeless house lots,
banks of fancy landscaped lawns,
creative glittering designs
hand-carved shapes with leaning ferns
a cuckold's prideful winning plan
chuckling nouveau manmade art,
a selling point to raise the rate
of expensive modern real estate.

First published in *Wolf Moon Down* by **Goose River Press**.

Diane H. Schetky
Topsham, ME

Where Have All the Words Gone?

Perhaps they are hiding in the woods,
playing hide and seek, like I did as a child,
then running wild through the trees.

Perhaps the words are adolescents
still dodging their chores, ignoring
the rules and trashing useful words.

Adult words scramble in Scrabble
where the I's prevail, but
not the tiles I am hoping for.

At times, my mind becomes
a traffic jam that slows down the
words called for or it sends them
on circuitous detours without
a GPS or map.

Today, I gave a museum tour to 2nd
graders and talked about whales.
I showed them some baleen
but the name for it escaped me.
I was rescued by a little girl
who announced it was "baleen!"

Some days, the words I need
go on strike and refuse to come
out, or worse yet, the wrong words
sprout such as Isis for Iris.
Are they competing for fresh air?

Diane H. Schetky
Topsham, ME

Some days, I think my mind
has run out of storage space or the
words are hiding in the attic of my mind
amidst the spider webs, dusty
remnants of organic chemistry,
physics and French, calculus and
Chaucer, fragments of Russian
and names of teachers long forgotten.

If only I could press a delete key
to evict them and allow more space
for the words and names I need.

***

Steve Troyanovich
Florence, NJ

the earth's fading psalm
for Ryszard Krynicki

dirge-like
the snow kept falling
on that late afternoon...
your refugee
wrapped in a plaid blanket
numb with despair
contemplated the constellations
of non-existent planets...
somewhere a little sparrow
shivers in the cold

Carolyn Locke
Troy, ME

What's Missing

Yesterday I watched heavy winds
churn the steel sky above the river,
and felt an emptiness
deep enough to lose myself,
which is maybe what I needed
to call back the familiar warmth
of my mother's hands,
the kindness in my father's eyes.

I never knew loss
could be so deep, so absolute,
that I would always
feel their presence the way an amputee
still senses cold in a missing limb,
that I would always be looking
for that lost part of myself.

And that's another thing: the way
one ache leads to another, the way
churning waters and naked trees
make me long for my children,
for the fullness of those bodies
once harbored safe within me.

As the winds die down, I turn
from the river, breathe in
the faint scent of fallen apples,
listen for the fading call
of wild geese swallowed by the sky.
The cold comes down sudden
and hard in the waning light.

Trudy Wells-Meyer
Scottsdale, AZ

You Must Have Been a Beautiful Baby
Denying the sadness of the world
would be denying the magnificence of the beauty
that exists in spite of it.

—Aryn Kyle

What does a husband feel, when hair flies off his adored wife's head, as she sits in a barber's chair, his barber for years, who uses a buzzer with its mosquito hum to destroy a dream hair cut in one agonizing instant? A style cut, given stares and compliments, from countless women, everywhere? His stomach turns. Fear for his wife he holds his breath, with a face of crushing sadness, possible tears? A volcano inside a husband's soul ready to erupt, his eyes stare at the floor covered with blond hair that means the world to his woman, his princess of forty harmonious years. His heartbeat desperately trying to match hers; an experience shared by few to live such a monster moment. In no time, a buzzer taking off a most beautiful shade of blond hair, hair that not only costs a lot, but is revitalized and paid for monthly. A shade achieved by Cara's favorite hair expert miraculously matching the hair color when Jonas and Cara met in the magical spring of 1951. A natural blonde when Jonas first set eyes on Cara, his date for the prom fifty-six years ago.

The cold hard side of life testing Jonas's love and smiley face as he watches Cara's trembling, unstoppable at the switch of the buzzer. In helpless terror Cara turns in the huge chair almost swallowing her slender body. Cara's regal air and sense of glamour deflated, not knowing what to say— knowing to say nothing—ready to scream. A husband and wife's eyes meet through a sea of shimmering tears as hair falls on the old worn tile; a giant moment in a wife's instant bald-head state. Jonas's face like a mirror utters magical

Trudy Wells-Meyer
Scottsdale, AZ

words, like an echo from across the room to break the eerie silence: "You must have been a beautiful baby. . ."

The power of words grew huge in a world without hair. A miracle no less something so ruined could shine; a life-altering event, the romance of it . . . what a sight into a husband's soul, one sizzling Arizona morning, as Jonas was forced to watch helplessly. The big C—cancer had called for his love. No more bad-hair days in Cara's life?

At Mayo Clinic located on the outskirts of Scottsdale, in the still blooming desert one cloudless day in early June 1991, at a doctor's office a husband and wife sat close to each other with worried faces, when a specialist, successful for 25 years, an oncologist announced the shattering news. The devastating news had hit their carefree life: lung cancer. (Later in the doctor's life, a cancer patient himself, he found out what survival really means and feels like.)

A desperate embrace of two people in shock was interrupted when a nurse with untidy, no-care-hair walked into the cold, typical Arizona over air-conditioned room. Cara and Jonas let go of each other, looked up and listened to the know-it-all nurse's unfeeling words: "Shave your hair! It will be easier than watching it fall daily."

One ghastly opinion, spoken by a nurse, who clearly encountered countless victims dealing with Cancer; how cruel to shave off anyone's hair, the pride and glory of women's existence. *Are there women who don't care?* Not to a hairdresser's knowledge. Unimaginable and an undeniable act of self destruction for a lady like Cara, with a unique air of elegance and glamour. A woman in the language and knowledge of couture, advised and helped by her own professional shopper.

> *You gain strength, courage and confidence by every experience in which you stop looking fear in the face . . . you must do the thing you think you can't do.*
> —Eleanor Roosevelt

Trudy Wells-Meyer
Scottsdale, AZ

Cara's desperate phone call to her much-loved hairstylist, one busy Friday morning at her esteemed salon will remain in my memory forever.

"Tyra, will you shave my hair off?" with a quiver in Cara's voice more like a whisper.

"Whaaaat?" I silently screamed. "Mrs. Jenkins, you want me to do what?"

With sinking disbelief, I winced, as if in pain. Overwhelming hurt surged for my favorite customer. *Shave off her beloved, attention-getting haircut; Cara's exceptional look, she called a masterpiece created for her only, different from all other women? How could I say no to one of my long-time clients in obvious agonizing pain?* Cara's panic-stricken voice saddened me immensely. If I could have cleared my mind of Cara's words and wished them gone then perhaps I could convince myself that they had not been spoken. They had. I took a deep breath, on the edge of decision, hesitating, I think I shouted: "Noooo! I don't think I can." The image of Cara's anguish dealing with the battle of cancer had me close my eyes. I listened to Cara's depressing news; my knees had gone weak. I reached for a chair.

"My husband's barber will," I heard Cara yell.

I grasped for my heart as to hold it not to burst. It seemed to have skipped a beat. *How can words hurt and help at the same time?* It was of gigantic importance and abundantly clear I had to help somehow. With a measure of hope a sudden thought had entered my mind. In mere seconds, I knew what to do. I tried to breathe; it was one of those moments where you could easily stop. I trembled as I mumbled, "I will help you find the perfect wig." Feeling a sense of relief, I now was crying behind my hand, when Cara uttered words I never thought I'd hear.

"I'll go to Jonas's barber. He listens. He will shave my hair." Click. The phone went dead.

My stomach felt like turning. I tried to compose myself. From numerous cancer-stricken clients I knew about the

Trudy Wells-Meyer
Scottsdale, AZ

unbearable methods to deal with this devastating illness. The ultimate agony . . . the no hair problem: Long hair does not look like cancer. No eyebrows left, hair ending up in hands, mostly in the shower, like an appearing monster scaring you. A picture with no frame. Nonetheless, I also knew, sometimes doctors were wrong, and some women's hair never fell out during chemo therapy that all depended on needed strength of treatments.

With a potent mixture of sadness, I convinced myself, a one-minute shave of a fashionable hairstyle, desired by various women, was not in my job description. Seeking joys of hair, I returned to the lady waiting in my chair, whose natural curls somehow looked more beautiful than before that sad call.

Years ago, when Mrs. Jensen first set foot into Mahogany's fancy salon in downtown Scottsdale, my racing thoughts of my busy schedule left me with anxious speculations. *Another new customer? Can I handle one more?* Knowing pressure is a privilege, I watched this sophisticated woman with a regal air look around and gasp at the number of clients waiting. I hoped it would scare her off. Cara ignored my worries. Each time of her appointment she brought a book and patiently waited her turn. A huge book on one of her visits I pointed to, shaking my head, "It won't take that long."

She smiled, even her eyes.

Cara Jensen's monthly visits included gossiping about her affluent circle of friends, family and bragging about her husband, Jonas. Laughter and interaction with countless customers and can-you-top-this story between women at the hairdresser's; hearing is believing. Smells of salon products and hair dyes possibly causing everybody to turn lightheaded, yakking and babbling even more.

Cara loved Mahogany's. A new salon, the talk of the town. A free-standing imposing building with an unusual layout; a sunken hair dryer area in the middle of the huge rectangular

Trudy Wells-Meyer
Scottsdale, AZ

room. Live plants, the rage of that era, decorated the corners and specific spaces. What a display of elegance; yet, its cozy appearance gave a feeling of home to a salon that was written up in the *National Hair Magazine* because of its uniqueness, serving men and women. Unisex, a new buzz in the seventies. My daily hair-heaven, back in the corner, consisted of two stations, a brand-new leather couch and three fashionable, comfy chairs along the wall for my customers to wait and be spoiled by my assistant Alena.

Mrs. Jensen's instant trust let me accomplish her own distinctive look. For years to come, we both received and experienced compliments, at times beyond comfort.

Cara lived the power of hair . . . hair is a feeling.

This woman simply was a stylist's dream customer, without the usual orders: not too short, cover my ears, leave the back long. Her one wish: no bangs. She adored one style that made me famous, a distinctive look, hair flipping away from the face undeniably added youth to any face; a bouffant, no-helmet-like hair-do with flair.

Cara kept her hair looking remarkable between visits. She was a walking advertisement. I marveled at her knowledge of style, desire of dressing classy, with utmost care; stared at and admired by clients at our hectic high-class salon.

In the life of hair designers, numerous times we feel the agony of unreasonable, never-making-sense wishes from demanding clients. They point to pictures, when all I think or reply: "I am a beautician not a magician."

Yet, Cara's look, magic of cutting emerged and my own eyes could hardly believe the capability of hair to astonish customers.

I lived for finding the perfect style for my clientele. I believed: Clients did not pay me for hair I cut off—they paid me for the hair I left on. My motto: *I don't cut hair to be short; I cut hair to look good.* Indelibly imprinted in my mind are the words of one of my customers for thirty-three years. At my

Trudy Wells-Meyer
Scottsdale, AZ

retirement party given by my clients, in a note she wrote, *"Tyra, you gave us what we didn't know we wanted."*

The dynamics of hair and bad-hair days returned to Cara's daily life. Pockets of paradise ignited a cloudy Arizona sky with ecstatic news: cancer free. Lung cancer, a statistical miracle, now twenty years! No more wig days that felt like a hat reaching her nose in frequent gusts of desert winds. Gone the days of a hairy hat that never allowed Cara to feel beautiful. A wig to cover her bald head during those difficult months; it simply made Cara feel self conscious and naked behind lifeless hair. Nevertheless, she admitted I managed to style her rag-wig almost striking.

Cara found a magical seed of gratitude, in a barber shop, one roasting Arizona morning. Words Cara would remember for the rest of her life: *You must have been a beautiful baby.* In Cara's darkest losing-her-hair-moments, the power of words, triggered a profound closeness to the man she proud-ly bragged about to anybody who would listen, "Jonas asks me every morning what I would like for dinner." *A cooking husband?* Jonas cooked daily for his wife after he retired. Through books, the internet, a billboard of knowledge and with the help of friends, Jonas and Cara learned about healthy cooking and eating. He admits: "We woke up. We now check and appreciate the value of nutrition."

Staying healthy is a skill.

Cara and Jonas believe, the world deserves to know, good nutrition can and does save lives. Health is a choice! Simply eat better—healthy choices.

Love is known to have no boundaries, what a treasure. A couple now for sixty years, they look at each other with eyes of immense love in a life for better and for worse. A marriage filled with a blaze of maybes when they were young; parents to one daughter who lives close by.

Cara learned the hard way; prayers carried her and Jonas. Nothing fuels a life quite like hope with the presence of God. *True happiness is to want what we have.* How we live

Trudy Wells-Meyer
Scottsdale, AZ

in our heads more than any place—aware of it more when things don't go well. What matters is the way we choose to remember how a whole life can come down to a single moment in June, one blistering Scottsdale day. We live for changes—how do we handle them?

Jonas and Cara now live up north, traded the big city life for the cool country, the Arizona woods where their dream house became reality, a long-time desire of the Jenkins. They truly live a life thankful for all things, unpretentious things; now stare at sunsets a little longer, when the sun turns an unusually deep color like an overripe orange falling from the tree to become part of the earth; a sky the colors of old china dishes. More than ever they feel the wisdom that sees the ordinary with amazement. Contentment is one of their greatest blessings.

This twosome knows comfort is luxury.

God with His heavenly source of unseen power fills the life of a marriage, joined through tragedy and helpless terror moments. A couple lifted from a spiraling freefall filled with hours of doctor visits and sleepless nights. Cara and Jonas learned health is their greatest wealth.

Cindy Partington
Dallas Center, IA

Reset

I'm tired of being
un
joyful

So, soften hard feelings
brood later
put off resentment
until I'm ready
not now
maybe never
Like Dad used to say
"There'll be time to be upset
when I'm dead."

Those pesky
downer messages
never give up
trying to worm their way
into my head
I know they're waiting
"under the radar"

Take last week's headache
my mental slings and arrows
are of no use
to deter or fix anything

Cindy Partington
Dallas Center, IA

Perhaps I shall
put having negative thoughts
on the bottom of my "to do" list
which grows longer and longer
and is regularly ignored because of
more pressing matters like

enjoying_______________

***

Sally Belenardo
Branford, CT

All That Remains

White moon, from the horizon pink,
through bare trees in twilight magically climbs,
possessing, still, its ageless powers
again and always to make me think
of you, these many years and hours
distant, seeing moonrise at different times.

Though once we shared its brightest phase,
the moon, like love, brought with it darkness, too.
Glimmers of heartache and rue appear,
wondering when or whether you gaze
on all that remains forever, Dear—
this moon—seen by me, and perhaps by you.

Jerry James Rempp
Reasnor, IA

Manger Child

You are the soft airy leaves
of spring ferns in shadowy woods
shrouded by sequin dewdrops
lying low against the breast of silent earth
beheld by the opening rays of morning
breaking through the milky mist

You are the loved One
poised breath and slumber of the infant
cradled from all effects,
save that of mother's fervent care:
That precious undisturbed presence
glowing bloom, pink and smooth,
closed tiny lids and lashes; chaste nostrils
cove to fresh and faultless lungs
and—as yet—unbroken heart

You are deep night sky
beckoning wonder beyond fulfillment
whose magic lies in ceaseless wonder:
The Pleiades, Aquarius, the evening
and morning Venus
reclining to Mars' adoring descent
smiled upon by the worn thin grin
of our own nocturnal Moon

You are moons and music,
children hopscotching innocence,
dreams of flight
at the top of the box elder tree;
Christmas scent under the living pine:
The manager child,
precious, atop the Baldwin piano
Mother played only in ragtime

Dawn Edwards
Ipswich, MA

A Mother's Pleasure

Tiny memories force their way into my mind slowly, dreamily as I gently fondle forgotten articles of an infant's wardrobe.

A beautiful, handmade christening dress lay creased and soiled in a dusty chest retrieved from the attic. As I unfold the precious item, it fills with life again, as I see my now seven-year-old son, as a sleeping lovechild, being held by his godmother. I watch him so trusting as the minister gives his blessing to the world's child of hope.

Narrow, white ribbons fall loose from the dressing gown, handed down through several generations, as I tenderly stroke its softness. It belongs in a bassinet surrounding a newborn, my newborn who has already found the pleasure and contentment of his thumb.

My thoughts, my memories engulf me now as they temporarily erase the present and I am once again the hesitant, unsure, proud, loving and undyingly faithful mother of the most beautiful child in the world.

***

Sylvia Little-Sweat
Wingate, NC

Dragonflies

With iridescent
oars dragonflies row Summer's
deep Sargasso Sea.

David Campbell
Somerville, MA

Window World

Looking for wholeness
    at my piece of window-world, I see
        the neighboring roofs grow cosmic, planetary,

as a trans-Atlantic contrail
    rises like a flying fish from the sea
        and glides across the glass as horizontally,

for a stretch, as horizons
    are supposed to be, then tilts
        its nose and plummets out of sight

toward LAX, O'Hare,
    I know not where, though west,
        behind suburban Belmont's wooded ridge—

a brilliant neon needle
    within the afterglow, its point
        avoiding sunset for passengers and crew

by streaking toward it
    faster than and counter to
        the planet's rotation into night;

their linear smoke signal
    telling me that paths of flight
        from point to point must orbit, bend.

Their day won't end
    until they stop pursuing it
        like mechanized moths, and land.

David Campbell
Somerville, MA

So the sky outside my glass,
   through which these high-flyers pass,
      confirms what Albert Einstein observed

and Galileo found—
   that space is curved
      and Earth is round.

***

A. McKinne Stires
Westport Island, ME

Close to Madness

Poetry arrives from the edge of madness,
an iron horse belching,
hot and black,
stinking of sweat,
writhing and pacing,
waiting impatiently
for a sigh or pounded fist
to validate its being.

Occasionally, poetry finds a crack
just wide enough to enter,
like Lady Beetles seeking warmth for the winter,
following pheromone clouds,
they roam the ceiling,
and collect in corners
near the attic window
waiting in safety and communion
for winter's madness to dissolve.

Gerald George
East Machias ME

Eminent Sense

What did he know, Don Quixote,
riding pack-saddle on the broken back
of a choked-up, spindle-riven horse, and worse,
accursed intellect immersed
in the fiddle-faddle of medieval sagas
of nit-witted knights-errant looking for other
tin-potted fools to swat.

Despite an overblown aspect of woe,
that spindly tilter at windmills knew
truth—to purse a significant life
you'd better forget your mind. Let it go!
Pay it no heed! For your grand ambition
assume—pretense! That is the source
of eminent sense!

Sancho Panza, the miasmic squire,
never recognized that. The fool,
wandered Spain on his spindly mule
behind the rainbow that glowed in the mind
of Don Quixote. But O Pancho,
how sensibly in the light of day,
seeing a danger, you ran away.

Tom Adamson
Fremont, NE

The Song I Never Wrote

It started long ago,
I recall the first note.
The one that got away,
The song I never wrote.

I feel the melody,
A tingle in my throat.
The one that got away,
The song I never wrote.

I'm one breath behind
Of a ghost that leaves no trail.
Just a trace of a song gone silent,
A shadow of a sun born pale.

The words I knew so well,
Once I could easily quote.
The one that got away,
The song I never wrote.

Stranded on a shore,
I never see the passing boat.
The one that got away,
The song I never wrote.

A stranger that I know,
So close yet so remote.
The one that got away,
The song I never wrote.

Patrick T. Randolph
Lincoln, NE

A Poem for My Wife

I wrote a poem for you and put it in my pocket,
Thought if I saw you in our kitchen or cleaning
Around the house, I'd pull it out and we'd have
Our own little poetry reading—just you and me.

I've kept it here now for almost a year, but the letters
Have all worn off and the paper's become a ball,
Almost as hard as a fossil loved by Time's whispers.
I hold onto it anyhow, waiting for that moment

When I can surprise you with a game of catch—
We will toss the poem back and forth, and let our
Laughter drip down on the moment like beads of rain
Euphorically lingering on the window long after the storm.

***

Images from Childhood
for my mother, Darlene

Father's tall, lean figure
Standing in the winter field;

He's looking up into the sky—
His ears and eyes listening to our
Ancestors' advice on

How to prepare for the coming storm—
The first snowflakes landing on his coat;
He turns, smiles, waves to me.

I walk toward my father—forever in
This Wisconsin morning memory.

Robert Erickson
Round Pond, ME

A Lucky Dog

It was December of 2016, and my wife Brenda and I were on our way to Arizona for the winter months, travelling from our home in Maine. We owned a condo in a small town called Fountain Hills which was close to Scottsdale. We had wintered there for years escaping the snow and cold after having retired. The trip was one we had made many times and we were very familiar with the route. We never stopped admiring and loving the absolute beauty of our country from beloved Maine through the Midwest lakes and cornfields, across the mighty Mississippi on to the expansive western states.

After stopping in Colorado to visit relatives, Brenda and I were on Interstate 40 , travelling through Santa Fe and Albuquerque, New Mexico, Then on to Gallup and crossed the Arizona border. The Native American influence along this stretch of America is spectacular. There are many roadside shops looking like teepees offering fine silver jewelry studded with turquoise and onyx. There were Kachina dolls, bows and arrows and feathered head bands for the kids. All very authentic.

The sun was low in the west, lighting up the magnificent crystalline cliffs of the Painted Desert. These are miles and miles of mesa rocks glowing with pinks, browns, reds and yellows. An unforgettable sight! The traffic was light so we could take in this beautiful arid desert scene and we found we were soon to be in the Petrified Forest National Park. The park is about 30 square miles of fallen trees that over more than thousands of years had transformed from wood to rock. As the wood disintegrated, it was replaced by rock and minerals. The trees had to have fallen in marshland for the moisture required for this process. We learned that this is the only place in the world where this had happened. Truly a sight to see.

Robert Erickson
Round Pond, ME

We continued our travel west in fairly light traffic at the speed limit. Ahead, there was a white pickup truck stopped in the breakdown lane and cars to our left. Being in the right lane, I slowed slightly to pass the pickup. Just then we noticed a dog in the grassy median that seemed very agitated. He was a good sized, white animal with large black spots, running back and forth from east bound to west bound and seemed to be wanting to cross our lane. I slowed more but just as I thought he was going to stay in the median, he ran across right in front of our car. I braked hard and veered to the right but "thud' we hit the dog with our left front fender. We heard and felt the impact and stopped immediately in the breakdown lane.

We felt terrible and ran back to the white pickup. There were three people in the front seat, two men and a woman in the middle. We told them how very sorry we were. They were obviously Native American and the male passenger told us that the dog was wild and belonged to Joe back up the road who never took good care of his dog. He said he couldn't take him back to the owner because Joe would accuse him of stealing his dog. It didn't make sense, but were just wondering what to do with this poor animal.

Just then two park rangers and a woman walked up having seen what had happened. We asked them what we could do with the dog as we had no room in our little car and didn't know where to go even if we had room. The woman said that there was a shelter in a town up ahead but the two rangers just looked down at their shoes and said nothing. We didn't know what else to say and we all just looked at each other. Then unbelievably the dog trotted from around the back of the pickup, wagging its tail and licking hands like a truly happy dog. We couldn't believe our eyes. Then, even more amazing, the dog reared back and leaped up through the open truck window and sat in the rear seat. Obviously it had been there before. That was enough for me and I said, "Let's go, Brenda." We drove the rest of the way to our condo and

Robert Erickson
Round Pond, ME

discovered a tear in our front bumper and the left fender was slightly buckled. A thousand dollar repair job later, we had our car back in shape. We still look back wondering what kind of a dog that was, but we do know one thing; that was one big, Lucky Dog!

***

Donna Bruno
Ft. Lauderdale, FL

Betsy Ross

As you diligently stitched by candle light,
Could you foresee the future symbolism of that unfurled
     banner?
     Rippling in the wind for all to see
First, a beacon welcoming immigrants to unfamiliar shores
     Later, above the sands of Iwo Jima, on Normandy
        Beaches,
Vietnam, Afghanistan and Iraq
     Wherever democracy was threatened
     Finally, shrouding the remains of courageous
        patriots
Who made the ultimate sacrifice.
     Stalwart, it waves lustily, defiantly in the fickle wind
Declaring that "all men are equal,"
        entitled to "liberty and justice for all"

Jean Lawrence
Waldoboro, ME

As I Age

As I age, death, with force and seeming regularity, intrudes
        into my life.
More and more often, it sweeps up a loved one, an old
        friend, or former student.
Even dear members of the community leave unexpectedly.

The tolling of time's bell rocks my being.
Nothing brings the reminder that I am a finite being like
        that of death's interruptions.
I am sad; I relive old memories; for a moment my steps
        slow.

I try to shake off the loss, but flashes of past moments
        persist.
I must call a halt to feeble attempts to avoid reality.
And so, I settle into grief, let its waves wash over me, and
        contemplate the future.

I must accept the close of a chapter in my book of life.
I must continue down the path of my own existence.
My story is not complete—only a kind of writer's block has
        halted the narrative.

In time, I pick up my living and move forward.
I do so emboldened with renewed faith and hope for the
        future.
My end is in sight, but my story is not finished!

Elmae Passineau
Weston, WI

The 1972 Schwinn

It was a beautiful thing, a gift,
bright green and shiny silver
and nary a spot of rust on the fenders
covering the sturdy thick tires,
all spokes intact,
seat and handlebars just right,
a reliable brake and oiled chains

But she hadn't ridden in twenty years,
the excitement
the anticipation
the trepidation were all there
as she straddled it and gripped the handlebars,
one foot on a pedal,
one foot anchored to the ground

Now or never
the right foot pushes on the pedal
the left foot rises from the driveway
taps the other pedal, finds it,
presses firmly,
it's moving, wobbling, straightening
and she's off—
down the driveway,
into the street,
around the corner, faster faster
feeling breeze-blown hair
and coolness in her face, a beautiful thing—
yes, yes, it's true what they say—
you never DO forget!

Sylvia Little-Sweat
Wingate, NC

Planting

In a stand of oaks
mourning doves called
across the field where
Daddy planted corn.
The mule, hitched to Grandpa's
planter, pulled Daddy like
a divining rod up furrows
that smelled of creek banks,
rain barrels set in houses' eaves,
dank hand-dug wells capped
with windlass, rope, and pail.

I panned the tow sack gold
with both small hands,
lugged bucketfuls up rows
on Daddy's command. As he
planted I bored bare toes
in cool black dirt then watched
them sprout like corn.

Crows cawed and caught
the draw with slanted wings.
At dusk Daddy led the mule
and me down the sawmill road
toward home. As the moon
broke the gathered dark,
dust-throated whippoorwills
from nests in distant fields
sang long elegies
to all life formed
from dust and seed.

Richard Manichello
Baltimore, MD

I Sell Clouds

He was a rangy, rust-colored waif, a floppy-eared numb-skull with droopy cheeks and sad brown eyes. He ate every-thing that came near his toothy slack jaw, the jaw with the wide red tongue constantly hanging out of it. He moved along this earth without a hint of any syncopated gait the Creator might have intended for four-legged creatures. He even tripped over his own feet (they didn't look at all like paws) and his flaccid frumpy ears slapped him in the face when he ran too fast. The dog couldn't see where he was going—damn-near killed himself, and my dad, a dozen times. He was a gangly critter.

On appearance alone, he could have set half-a-dozen pure breeds back centuries on the evolutionary charts. He and my father were inseparable. Most of the time, it was hard to tell who was looking after whom.

Heyyou was a ratter. He would sniff-out rats down on the river bank, and my father and his cronies would shoot them with their *lupari*, their Sicilian rifles. It was sort of a poor man's fox hunt, without the horses, or the pinks, or a fox. My father called the dog Heyyou because it was simple and uncomplicated. It had a "ring of authority," my dad said.

"Heyyou, c'mere, Heyyou, siddown!"

A man has to assert his authority when dealing with ani-mals, my dad always told us, like he was some trainer, or dog whisperer, or something. He found the dog hiding in the wood stacks over in Mariotti's lumber yard. Heyyou looked awful, cowering and moaning. So many things were living in his brown knotted coat he could have charged rent. He looked like he had been beaten, too. I remember my dad had some tears in his eyes when he was washing him down in the warm water and the Duz detergent, in our backyard, in the big green washtub. Heyyou never flinched. The way my dad

Richard Manichello
Baltimore, MD

was stroking him with his big rough hands, it must have been very reassuring to that desperate animal.

My father wrapped him up in one of Mom's big blue bath towels to dry him off, rubbing him slowly so he wouldn't get frightened. About a dozen kids from the neighborhood, and my brother and me, stood and watched the whole affair, listening to my father talk about dogs like he was a professional breeder, or something. That old dog just shivered and looked at my dad the whole time—the two of them staring at each other like movie stars. My dad kept kneading his boney frame gently, patting him dry. I think my dad had some tears in his eyes. It was that or it might have been the Duz soap.

The event was exciting enough to take-up the whole afternoon watching, and half of the next day talking about it. No one ventured a guess at the dog's previous-but-unknown name, so my father decided it'd be less confusing and *easier on the dog* to give him a simple sounding name. My father gave that dog a simple name because anything new we might've attached to that canine would have taxed my father's memory, and for memory, my father had a mind like a sieve. His absent-mindedness was legend.

***

The Lackawanna Line of the Blue Ridge Valley Trolley Car Company ran down the center of Main Street, right in front of our house, and it stopped no more than fifty feet from the front porch. My father stood one day, directly across the street, waiting for the southbound trolley to Nanticoke. The new Chevys had just come out—he was a Chevy man, my dad—and he and a couple of the fellas from up-the-line were going to the Chevy dealer in Nanticoke to see the new models, first-hand. He was standing at the trolley stop, talking to Giacometti, the butcher, and Marianelli, the shoemaker.

You see, in our town, any fella standing on Main Street for more than about twenty seconds was reason enough for

Richard Manichello
Baltimore, MD

some other fella to assume that *that* fella, the one standing there, wanted to talk—about anything. It was sort of an unwritten code. Our Main Street had groups of men standing, and talking, on just about every corner, sometimes in-between corners, almost any time of the day or night, anytime of the year, except when it rained. When it rained they went inside and played poker, and talked. So, after the prescribed twenty-second waiting period, you could have yourself a gathering of two or more men on Main Street. You might see, in places, anywhere from three to fourteen fellas standing there, on the sidewalk, blabbing away, yelling and hollering about far-ranging topics in colorful discourse, talking in various tongues, gesturing and cussing in a variety of languages—men just talking, in groups, anywhere from five minutes to three or four hours.

They say that my father barely took a breath that morning, in the passion of the all-important argument. They say, he was going on and on about Virgil or Verdi, or Shakespeare, or General Motors, nobody remembers for sure, and he was getting all worked-up in the *discussing.*

The trolley car came. The captain rang a bell, and the trolley car left. My father never got on. He was on the sidewalk talking until noon. My mother and several other women on the street watched in amusement from their shady porches, just shaking their heads.

My father taught English at our high school, after he quit the coal mines. We think he was the original Absent-Minded Professor. My brother and I called him that. The classic case came some years later. It was the time my father drove the car into the city, and took the bus home. Believe it. It became our town's favorite fable.

He went to an Army-Navy store, over in Southside. He left the car in the parking lot, then took the Gray Line, Number Seven bus back home. He probably jingled the car keys in his pocket all the way back on the bus. My mother was waiting in the kitchen when he came in. He beamed about the won-

Richard Manichello
Baltimore, MD

derful day he had spent in the city, went on in detail about how the people strolled the avenues all dressed in crisp clothes—the women in starched long skirts and the men in their wide-brimmed Stetsons and fedoras and skimmers. My mother listened. My brother and I stood on the rungs of the rocking chair, by the refrigerator, and watched this nattily-dressed thespian put on his *Commedia dell arte* for us.

My mother had a sinister smile twitching beneath her glare, as she stood in her apron by the stove. My mom had two smiles—one was made of brown sugar and love, the other was pure vinegar. She had a little of both in-reserve for my father's grand operas. The big wooden spoon was raised on high and she began to lead an imaginary orchestra to my father's aria of the big city. The water in the big pot on the stove began to boil gently, and a rich red sauce made syncopated plopping sounds from the flat black pan on the back burner. With the choral section and the orchestra going full-steam behind her, she listened and conducted the kitchen symphony to my father's recitative. Her smile broadened as he came to the bombastic finale of his ode to the beautiful city. And, with a curly-cue motion of the wooden spoon, conductor and tenor ended the opera buffa in perfect unison. My brother and I clapped raucously, feeding my father's bravado, urging him on. He took his bows, and we all showered him with enthusiastic applause.

Then came my mother's bombast.

"*Marmoto!* When are you going back to the beautiful city for the car?"

"*O'Mamma mia!* I left the damn car at the store." He shouted, slapping himself on the forehead with his big meaty hand, and retrieving the clinking keys from his pocket.

By now, my brother and I were on the floor, barely breathing in our hysteria. We feared my mother's wooden spoon would descend upon us for our mockery, but our laughing was uncontrollable. We never got the spoon, however, it was only meant to be a deterrent, and the threat was

Richard Manichello
Baltimore, MD

warning well-enough. In all the times I can remember of my father's forgetful adventures and misadventures, usually all four of us lowered the final curtain laughing. My father laughed the loudest.

"*Checo*," my mother would say, tapping his forehead with her flour-covered thumb. "In here, you have clouds, big puffy white clouds. If I could sell clouds, *Checo*, I'd be a very rich woman."

My father would shyly rub the cloud of flour dust from his forehead with his sleeve.

"Teresa" he'd murmur awkwardly, and somehow my mother's name had more syllables than Constantinople. "I was thinking of something important on the bus ride home. Something I wanted to say to my class, something I wanted to write, something poetic."

"You're a dreamer, *Checo*. A real dreamer." She'd smile, and then lean over and give him a kiss on the top of his head. He always looked like a third-grader when she kissed him like that. My father stood grinning sheepishly, and she would spin around to the bubbling cacophony on the stove, turn a few dials, drop a small handful of salt into the boiling water, and speak to the rising steam that billowed toward the ceiling,

"So, when are you going for the car?"

He'd put his tan Borsalino back on, tilt it to one side, curve the brim down just right with a flick of his thumb and forefinger, and walk gingerly out the door to sit on the porch. He'd just sit there and watch the trolley cars and count the new Chevys going by on Main Street, until dinner was on the table.

***

My father found a dog and called him Heyyou. He said it would be easier on the dog. A complicated name, on top of his own, might confuse the poor animal. My father knew

Richard Manichello
Baltimore, MD

something about confusion. He had a giant-sized compassion for men and beasts, favoring the beasts, I'm sure. People everywhere loved him—they revered him like some character out of mythology, or the Sunday comics. The men on the street corners, and in the beer-gardens, and at the poker tables, still tell stories of my father's absent-mindedness, his fantasies and his comical eccentricities. The stories get grander with each telling.

I suppose it is an act of love and some reverence that aggrandizes truth into myth. The town myth goes: his funeral procession was the largest ever, in the biggest blizzard, during the coldest February anyone can ever remember. People back home never checked records, they counted cars. And the long, unbroken line of cars that trailed his hearse that cold day ran the length of Main Street, stretched all the way down Drakes Lane, past The Breakers, and right on up to the Cumberland Street Cemetery—and it gets longer and longer as the years pass. As we age we diminish, only our story gets larger.

Heyyou died exactly ten days after my father was buried. He roamed around the house, and the backyard, looking for those big meaty hands that stroked his shiny brown fur. Every day at five-o'clock, he curled-up under the chair where my father read the newspaper. He'd lie there and stare at the pair of empty slippers on the footstool in front of the chair. Sometimes, I'd come running in from baseball practice, lie down on the carpet and just watch that old dog. He'd look at me, and I was sure then, as I am now, that God peers-out through the eyes of sad creatures. The species of the earth may be separated by light-years of intelligence, but the pain in that dog's eyes, an ineffable vision of sadness that I can never forget, spoke to all living things of the vast amounts of hurt in the world. Heyyou's face and my father's empty slippers became symbols of loneliness and loss in my memory forever. Two souls had parted ways, it seemed, and now searched an ever-widening void for reunion.

Richard Manichello
Baltimore, MD

For ten days, Heyyou waited and finally realized that my father wasn't coming home to fill those worn-out slippers, or touch his soft brown fur. Both men and beasts will perish in an absence of love.

We put Heyyou in that old green washtub, wrapped in a big blue bath towel, and buried him up on Fennel Hill. My brother and I, and about two dozen kids from the neighborhood, performed a brief ceremony behind the garage. Then, single file, our procession line walked solemnly down by the river bank, then, past the lumber yard, and finally, made the long cold climb up the Hill where we laid him in a grave chiseled out of the frozen ground with a pickaxe. It was the biggest dog funeral ever—about twenty-five or thirty of us— on one of the coldest days in February. Nobody ever disputed that.

*****

From the top of Fennel Hill, where we buried Heyyou, I can see our old house. I can see the front porch. Mariotti's lumber yard is still there. It's a lot bigger now, and the river bank is all green with new grasses. The trolley cars are gone, but groups of men still gather on Main Street, on the corners, and sometimes in-between, still talking, endlessly talking about everything. And right from this spot, where we laid that old dog down, I can see the Cumberland Street Cemetery and my father's grave. And, I guess, maybe it was only seven or eight kids for Heyyou's funeral that day, and my brother and me. It seems like there were a lot more.

Karen E. Wagner
Hudson, MA

Poseidon's Sigh

I walk the puddles and
feel the wind in my face
that makes me hurry to keep pace
with the waves as they pound
the beach and sound
like hollow barrels being struck
with the breadth of Poseidon's sigh.

I go down to the docks
to feel the pulse of the sea
and soak that rhythm into me.
As the tide comes in,
brings the fleet boats and fishermen,
who unload the gaping mouthed fish
with bulging eyes
slithering from the net to die
to be called fresh
catch of the day
market ready, straight from the bay.

Our life's a skiff
cut loose on the sea.
Verses of this poem anchor me,
give meaning
to the years gone by
help shape the future as she flies
to the call of the cormorants' cries.

Robert B. Moreland
Pleasant Prairie, WI

Somewhere West of Muskegon

Through bitter chill of night, he waits for her
though spring's nativity may never come.
Waxing Snow Moon with silvery ice ring
peeks through the translucent clouds with pale light.
Winter was early this year, gray squirrels'
bushy tails foreboding storms. December
gales battered the beach, piling up ice floes.

In his mind, she peers across a great lake
somewhere west of Muskegon, there on shore
twelve miles south of Wind Point to a cottage
where lights burn wicks of hope in the window.
Summer's verdant foliage hid the view;
now winter's naked hardwoods unashamed
usher light onto undulating waves.

Nascent apple tree blooms wait patiently
for red wing blackbirds who will herald spring.
*Will she come in time for the pastel fields
of shooting stars in May?* He lost his heart
to freckled faced romance one warm August
when cicadas and crickets offered song
as the Morning Star breached the prairie sky.

Now he waits, somewhere west of Muskegon,
far from her Berkshire hills. He knows that spring's
resurrection will only bring heartbreak.
The lights exhaust themselves, puddles
of wax, dreams dissolve to reality
as cold as a northeast wind off the lake.
With a sigh, he releases the vain hope.

Cindy Partington
Dallas Center, IA

Imprints

the only indentations
in an expanse of fresh snow
my crisp clear footprints
irrefutable evidence
recording my presence
here and now
in a white wonderland
with forgotten realities
lying temporarily underneath

by mid-day
the record has been altered into
irretrievably sunken and blurred
misrepresentations
my path has
melted into its surroundings

by dusk
the stringy record
is locked in icy semi-permanence

memories too
slowly merge and disappear
from consciousness
and our shared reality is
slowly reshaped, hidden, replaced
with new realities

most memories melt away into the background
or freeze somewhat distorted—
parts exaggerated, parts left out

Cindy Partington
Dallas Center, IA

a few forever memories
pack never dissipating
never-ending
images with
razor sharp edges

***

Carolyn Locke
Troy, ME

In Two Worlds

Now earth has turned just enough
for sunlight to glisten dew-wet branches

and find its way through the window
to this body, hungry for something

beyond itself, these hands cradling stones,
these fingers seeking with each firm stroke

the essence of island in Newfoundland's
glossy black, Iona's rough-hewn heart.

We know little of stones, and yet today,
today these stones are singing

a wilderness of far-flung light
piercing the thin veil between us.

the late Esther Ellen Dorr
Cumberland, ME

Tragedy

We saw our love shine in the night,
A candle flame
So small and bright.

But other lights
Burned all about—
How could we see
Our light go out?

***

Andrea Suarez-Hill
Jonesboro, ME

Monday

March wind spins dead leaves,
spruce trees sound their whistle
to a steel gray sky that
hangs its girders low,
smothers sun's rise,
blackens bay's green glass
under cumulous pillows
weightless, snowy shades
that billow, unfold and bend,
Nature's nurse who
asks her patient,
Man-worn poor,
to rise once more.

Bobby A. Troutt
Gallatin, TN

The Last Bloom of Summer

Summer, summer, o' summer, how quick you have come and gone. For, when I was a child, long ago, your long hot days comforted me and brought me so much joy as I played. Your joy in the early morn of the sounds of the birds singing unto the Lord was so comforting. Your warm but short summer rains helped bring relief on a hot day. Your clear and bright sky of blue, bare feet, dirt roads and playing in the creek all the day long enhance the memories of my childhood (that will always be so true). I remember catching lightning bugs on your warm long summer nights as Mom and Dad sat on the porch enjoying their rest from a long hard day of work. At night as I slept by an open window, I listened to the crickets, the sounds of frogs in a nearby pond and the lonesome cry of a whippoorwill many times before I went off to sleep. So simple of a life during the simple times of long ago. That brings me so much joy and peace in my days of old. The little and simple things always meant the most to me. They have brought me through my life's seasons (God has blessed me with). Summer, summer, how quick the time goes. As the last bloom of summer closes and fades away unto the bright brilliant colors of the autumn trees. Autumn, autumn, I love you, too. Your crisp and cool breeze, the smell of the burning leaves and the sound of the geese flying south above me brings back many memories (for God has been so good to me). The hauling of hay, tobacco hanging in the barn, foggy mornings, pumpkins in the fields, the gathering of corn and the cutting of wood; some good memories, some not so good. Oh, yes, I almost forgot. O' Tom Turkey, homemade dressing and giblet gravy and all our blessings, too (for young and old) from our awesome God who loves us so. We have so much to be thankful for.

Trick or treat, I guess you would say there's still a little

Bobby A. Troutt
Gallatin, TN

mischievousness in me. Autumn, how quick you have gone with the last of the falling leaves that bare the nakedness of the trees as the cold of winter moves in. As I remember as a child, the winters were as cold as they are to me now, but I always found delight in the fallen snow. The smell of cedar always brought back so much joy to me. The memories of sitting by the fireplace with Grandma and Grandpa on a cold winter's night eating walnuts and hickory nuts by the fire as the sound of the seasoned wood sizzled and popped. What a joy it was at Christmas being together with all your family and all your cousins, too. Laughing and sharing memories of years ago, with the family tree dressed and adorned with all our gifts nestled under the tree (with the anticipation of the coming of O' St. Nick). We listened to the songs of the season and the songs of the birth of Jesus, my Lord and Savior, the true meaning of Christmas; it's not about what you get but He that was given. Now that I'm old and alone, memories of the little and simple things mean so much to me. Winter has come and gone with the last melting snow and the opening of the new buds of spring. (God has been so good to me.) Do I need to say anymore?

***

Sylvia Little-Sweat
Wingate, NC

Phoenix

Smoke feathered her arms
and hands as she stoked the fire—
old crow hunched in cold.

Laureen Haben, osf
Milwaukee, WI

Remembering Grandma and Grandpa

Memories pop into my head in scattered order.

I would vacation a week on the farm. I knew how to feed the chickens, fill the mason jars with water and turn them upside down so the chickens could drink.

I would grind the hard corn kernels from the cob in a grinding machine. Grandma had a grinding machine too, but it was to grind the coffee beans into granules.

When it came to Saturday night baths, that was really different. You see, Grandma and Grandpa had no indoor bathroom so Grandma put a wash tub in the kitchen, filled it with water and gave me my bath.

Sunday mornings were special. We went to church and I sat in the choir with Grandpa because he was a singer.

Sunday afternoons were special, too. Every Sunday Daddy drove us from Niles Center to Northfield to visit Grandma and Grandpa. If Daddy was busy at home, he went back until after supper when he came to get us. In very cold weather he always warmed the car before we got in.

Summer Sundays found the aunts and uncles joining us on the front porch, some on chairs and some sitting on the steps

Thanksgiving Day was filled with lots of smells. The kitchen was steamy with all kinds of holiday smells, of turkey, stuffing, sweet potatoes, cranberries and pumpkin pie. Grandma was busy and Mother always brought some things to help with the meal.

Christmas was celebrated, not at Grandma and Grandpa's but at our home. One memory pops out. Mother and Grandma were speaking something in German, a thing I didn't ever remember happening before or again. Nosey teen Helen, knowing no German, figured out that Grandma asked Mother if I believed in Santa Claus. Apparently, Mother did

Laureen Haben, osf
Milwaukee, WI

not know, for I was wise enough to never speak my thoughts
on the subject. As far as I was concerned, there was always
a Santa Claus in our house.

That memory tops them all!

***

Paul G. Charbonneau
Rockport, ME

Birds of a Feather

Why oh why, lord goldfinch,
did you hightail it away
when the princely cardinal
perched where you were feeding?

Surely you hunger as much as he.

His masked face ruffled your feathers?
Or did you fly off plainly afraid,
seeing he was bigger than you?
It's a lot like that where I feed too.

Ann Pike
Wilton, ME

Wine, Whine and Age

Somehow without exactly knowing when, decades of rac-ing full-speed ahead like a time piece wound too tight have caught up with me. My gears are showing wear, although I am not yet ready to replace any cogs.

I wanted to age with grace and dignity. Instead I spend my days doing a little of this and a little of that and a whole lot of what might be considered whining.

In the morning I meander down fourteen narrow stairs, having learned since falling a couple of times to keep one hand on the banister for balance and my eyes tilted down-ward. Determined, I make sure each thick-soled shoe with its uncomfortable orthopedic insert arrives as planned on the appropriate descending step. I should be grateful that I can still navigate the stairs and don't have to install a chair lift, but I am not filled with gratitude, just whines.

Next in my day comes a short sprint on the training bike to get the heart rate up and the knees working with me. I sweat to the point where my cotton turtleneck sticks to my back. After ten minutes worry starts to cycle too, thoughts of selling the condo and moving to an apartment, one floor with rooms strung together like lines of profanity uttered in anger.

I say, "Enough."

I'd rather sip coffee and watch cable news, full of politics guaranteed to get the energy flowing. Now that I am all fired up about the Russian hacking, Trump tweets, a deep state, and untethered truth, I climb the stairs before lunch to write a few pages of a memoir that will probably never cross any agent's desk.

While making lunch I notice, with an aging mind that often loses focus, the dark spots on the glass stove top. I take time to clean the heating rings before washing dishes from the day before or maybe even the day before that. I don't real-

Ann Pike
Wilton, ME

ly remember. Finally I remove my sandwich that is still in the microwave, the timer having beeped 5 minutes ago.

During lunch I watch confirmation hearings. Hopefully I can watch and eat without heartburn, since my grilled chicken sandwich is smothered with melted horseradish cheddar whose pungent bite will bring tears. Just in case, the Tums already sit on the table beside two books articulating the craft of memoir.

Afternoons usually bring a choice of strolling down the driveway or revising the wonderings of my mind, scratched earlier when I was fired up. Maybe on this day I'll read some soothing passages from one of five books that hold my short attention span, each with a stylish bookmark as a reminder of where I left off. The choice depends on whether I take a nap or how I feel without an additional shot of cable news, which is becoming more depressing with each view.

At 4:45 p.m. I go outside, start the car, and drive three miles to get the mail. By now the hour closes in on dinner and raises the question of what to serve myself.

Not wanting to open another can of Healthy Choice Soup, I spend sixty minutes going through recipes cut from magazines, bought for their pictures of stylish homes and meals. I find a recipe, Hunger Ender Soup, which looks healthy enough to go with my goblet of wine, one tonight not two. I check the ingredients to see if all required items for this gourmet delight are sitting on shelves in my refrigerator or cupboards.

Of the ingredients listed I find one missing item, frozen peas, the main ingredient. "That figures," I snort.

I wish I had thought about dinner earlier before driving three miles into town. Then I could have stopped and shopped at the corner store. I am tempted to go out again, but the cold has immobilized me. I return to the recipe pile and settle on a second choice, Stress Soother.

After dinner I call my daughter to check in and let her know that I have not fallen today and am doing well. It is not

Ann Pike
Wilton, ME

a requirement, but a habit of mine to make a human contact at least once a day, a contact beyond the strangers I say hello to in the post office or corner store.

At 8:30 p.m. I head upstairs, an easier trip than going downstairs. I slide into comfy XXL leopard print PJs, the latest fashion, and snuggle into bed with the Kindle. I expect to watch an hour of my favorite, PBS Masterpiece Theater, but tonight the mercurial mind switches, and I read the Kindle version of How to Show Your Work by Austin Kleon.

After twelve hours of restless sleep, I rise to meet the new day. It ends up looking pretty much like the day I just finished. I am not sure if this is a comforting routine, or if like cable news, I am heading for depression. Who knows?

I think I am doing well. I do not require any major changes, having aged myself thirty years beyond the oldest edible commercial cheese in the world, a forty-year-old cheddar. It's maker claims that this cheese should be taken only in small doses, a reminder to me that I too should take everything in small doses: wine, self-pity, aging, and even cable news.

***

Patrick T. Randolph
Lincoln, NE

September Sonnet

Raindrops—
    coherently chattering
    on the kitchen
    windowpane.

*Based on work by Nina Radulovic

A. McKinne Stires
Westport Island, ME

The River Begins and Ends in Still Water

Our canoes drift with the current
of the ancient stream, tea-colored
and sheltered by leafy arches
in sifted sunlight
dipping nearly to the water—
arms with crooked fingers
guarding mossy banks
as if to say, "We protect you."
A carillon of thrushes ruffles
the hush of beech and birch,
a kingfisher flits on her well-worn perch,
her twitter sticking to the echoes.

The river flows with greater purpose, now,
lifting mud and sand,
leaving pebbles and cobble,
ripped from mountains eons ago,
rolling and bumping their way to roundness
to settle here, to disorganize the water's course.
Bush roots and tree roots
dangle from scoured banks.
Sounds in the sylvan glade fade
as we guide our way through burbling eddies
directing our watchful eyes forward,
not knowing what obstacle might come next.

Shining white granite boulders
as big as horses, litter our way,
gleaming in spray-misted sunlight,
like immovable tug boats headed upstream,
their bows forcing water to bend to their will.

(continued)

A. McKinne Stires
Westport Island, ME

Choices must be made.
Which side is wrong?
The river answers for me.
You make your own way through
this tempestuous chaos.
Our many forays downstream
taught us the path to the safety of the shallows.

We have read river's message.
We know how near lie the falls.

***

Susan van Alsenoy
Wiscasset, ME

Beaver Moon

The waxing Beaver Moon takes brittle bites out of the knife
    cold, sharp night sky.
It feeds its orange belly full of light to make nocturnal
    hunting an easy grasp.
It sees the rivers start to freeze as the earth puts on a coat
    of frost.
It knows its namesake is ripe for trapping, its body for fat,
    food, and fur,
       supplies to weather the Winter Moon ahead.

Robert B. Moreland
Pleasant Prairie, WI

Addie

Hard of hearing, she awoke to yell her good morning
until a little embarrassed toned it down. I was hers.
Forget marital bonds. She inhabited my chair, kept watch;
mourned when I was away, rejoiced when I came home.

Most precious, she'd call me to bed until I complied
and in her place between our pillows would wait
until my face turned to her and eyes closed,
she would put her own head down and sleep.

Mortality is the curse in a fallen world. At nineteen
she was a hundred and forty. Cataract clouded eyes,
Lauren Becat pleas and a weak, insistent purr.
In March she began to fade, unable to care for herself.

With difficulty she walked. I loved her all the more.
The dreaded day came, oh God why, drive to the vet.
When at last she could not go on, I stroked her head
told her of my love and let her slip from this life.

Addie, I pray the lion and the lamb are real,
when God calls me home, I see you at the gate
healed, young again with those deep green eyes
clear at last, gravelly meow of "What took you so long?"

Jeanne Severin-Hansen
Knightdale, NC

Summer Vacation

Every fall we returned to school with a reluctance known only to children. We were sorry to see the end of fireflies, sunsets that went forever stretching across the horizon and melting upwards to meet the first evening star. Every fall brought the dreaded assignment, My Summer Vacation. This was a perennial favorite of teachers. Either they can't think of anything else to assign or they are looking to see what the children in their class retained from the year before. I wonder how many papers said the same thing. I went swimming. I visited my relatives in Outer Babadock. I read a book. The eyes of countless teachers' glaze over as they read what the student thought teacher wanted to hear. Yet this scene was repeated September after September.

No one ever really told the truth in those essays. They wrote what they thought the teacher wanted to hear. They never told what their summer was truly like. The girl who spent the summer on the backyard swing while her father and Uncle Boo played poker in their undershirts. The boy who hid in the garage while his parents drank beer and tended bar at night never said so on paper. The one who told of attending a poetry intensive at the local library for three weeks, who read to the blind lady down the block once a week was firmly told not to make stories up and given an F. Too many students were placed in the untenable position of inventing something, lying to keep up an appearance of normalcy. Instead of telling the truth they were left feeling inadequate. Different was discouraged in those days of conformity. Revelation of any possible abusive situation or individual problem was not something the teacher wanted to deal with back in the 1950s. Every year those papers came back liberally marked up with red pen. It's a small wonder so many children would rather go to the dentist than back to school

Jeanne Severin-Hansen
Knightdale, NC

in September.

Today we have television that celebrates the same era through a different lens sliding us back into *Happy Days, The Wonder Years, Marcus Welby, MD* and many others.. For those of us who lived during those years the television sitcom glosses over so much, Hollywood lending its unreality to what we knew. We were much more free then, and exploration was a part of each day. Today people would call us free range children and concerned neighbors would call CPS and report our parents as neglectful. The constant need to entertain children today, keep them regimented and over-supervised seems just as odd to me as my childhood seems to many raising children today.

I think of those days now, and how it felt to pack my bags for the annual trip out to our maternal grandparents' home. It took a long time then, there was no Long Island Expressway or four lane Sunrise Highway. There was only Montauk Highway winding its way along the south shore from our home to freedom and the Shinnecock Hills. The constraints of school fell away behind me with each passing mile and the joy of summer began when we jumped out of the car and ran to our cottage.

Every summer we spent out on The Hill with our cousins. Oh yes, The Hill. The magical compound set in the midst of the Shinnecock Hills just outside Southampton, NY. Southampton then was not what people see today, full of wealthy movie and Broadway stars, the playground of the ultra-rich. While there was a great deal of wealth there, it was of a more modest sort and definitely more discrete. For us, it was a place free of structure where imagination was encouraged and play was the order of the day—all day. My grandparents lived in The Big House, an unpretentious ranch built in the 1950s after my grandfather retired. We lived in a one room cottage with no television, and no telephone and a sink that had a hot and cold water tap that both dispensed cold water. My mother heated up water on the

Jeanne Severin-Hansen
Knightdale, NC

stove and we took our baths in the sink behind a beach blanket mother held up for privacy.   Our cousins lived in their own cottage, which sorted a separate bunk room. We were close enough to our cousins' to hear if they were awake and had finished breakfast without looking out our window into theirs. We all ran across the hill to our grandparents' basement to use the one bathroom. Anyone approaching the bathroom made a great display of knocking politely to ascertain if it was free or occupied. We didn't have any set schedules, no cut in granite rules, but we learned to respect the privacy of others then. We learned early on that good manners got us respect and respect got us the privilege of having relatives that were also dear friends.

For years we took Red Cross swimming lessons.   We walked down the dirt road singing Ricky Nelson songs while looking for nesting quail or the occasional rabbit. A school bus took us to the Shinnecock Canal for those lessons and then brought us back home for lunch and flat-on-bunk reading time. We ran around barefooted, carefree and largely unsupervised. We had more time for play then, a magical time where we invented our own lives, fell out of trees and learned a bit of astronomy at night as we lay on the grass gazing at a vast sky. This was not neglect, benign or otherwise. It was the best thing that caring adults can do for children—provide them with the time to be children and learn by doing.

We painted rocks long before the invention of Pet Rocks. We made up and performed our own plays. One year a one ring circus came to town. We watched the big tent go up and walked the mid-way before it was officially open. The next week we performed in our own circus, our parents paid admission and sat in chairs on the lawn.

There were summer rains and enormous thunderstorms. The rain water washed down the hill and ran into our cottage, to be soaked up by our beach towels, and wrung out in the kitchen sink. Those summer storms brought an after-

Jeanne Severin-Hansen
Knightdale, NC

math of childhood delight. There were puddles to splash in and one such puddle so large we called it Lake Louise. We made our own armada of ships from bits of wood and rags tied to a nail mast. There were no mud pies or other bits of childhood domesticity. We were four girls inventing our future as pirates, America's Cup skippers and naval admirals. Who in their right mind would make a mud-goo pie when they could be an admiral for a few hours? We'd splash and salute and laugh. Laughing was an integral part of our summer days and nights.

We swam in the ocean almost every day while we were in elementary school and every day once we got into high school. If we weren't swimming we were taking long runs or hikes where ocean waves met the land. We were healthy, strong and tanned by the end of August. I loved those days at the ocean, the life guards and other people enjoying the summer sun and the leisure to talk with people that I had grown close to through years of shared experience.

I am not entirely sure what a teacher would think about a second grader telling her that children learned better by playing, and that getting our feet wet and muddy was much more than "just being naughty." I'm sure the essay would be marked up with lots of red ink telling me I didn't know what I was talking about, that imagination was no substitute for good grammar and I should pay attention during arithmetic lessons. We sat at our desks in long rows facing the chalk board. The teacher held a ruler and faced us with a face that spoke of disapproval and threat. We would all learn our lessons at the same speed and do as we were told.   Children were rarely listened to then, and received little to no respect as individuals. Teaching methods are much improved now, and much healthier for student and teacher alike. I think teachers still ask for an essay on What I Did For Summer Vacation. I hope they take the time to hear what the child is saying and leave their red pens' judgments in the trash can.

Sylvia Little-Sweat
Wingate, NC

Serenity

Still and gray as winter oaks at day
Each doe is hidden in the gloom.
Rain glazes brown leaves.   My
Every step marks the dark of trees,
Nothing to part the gray but wary
Deer flicking tails like white flags
In surrender for a moment then
Poised to flee. Each watches me,
Invokes a birthright to wilderness,
Trades vigilance for a brief unity,
Yields a silent legacy, then flees

***

Poppies

Blood of Tuscany
etches sienna skylines—
September sunset.

***

Lavender

In cottage gardens
lavender distills Summer
to last until Spring.

Carolyn Locke
Troy, ME

Premonition
for Tanya

Geese are flying
      through my dreams,
           first in a long, trailing V,

then a large swirling circle
      of gabbling and honking
           spiraling in on itself,

to a tight pulsing orb.
      Something precious
           I sense

is being held
      at the center—
           but before

I can grasp a thought
      beyond feeling,
           a lone goose

breaks free
      and drops to the ground.
           She stands before me,

shapeshifting—
      now a red fox
           with black tipped ears.

Her golden eyes
      gaze into mine
           for one brief moment.

Carolyn Locke
Troy, ME

Then she turns,
      disappears into the woods,
            and I wake

to the emptiness
      of your leaving
            before you have gone.

***

Robert B. Moreland
Pleasant Prairie, WI

First Light

I dreamt of you last night before morning
wisps of daybreak came. Your hazel eyes still
sparkle, silver strands among chestnut cling
to a freckle-faced countenance. Smile until
we embrace, four decades past. I take in
your warm softness then feel your heartbeat. We
chat, just small talk; catch up. Then, I begin
to capture your essence in this moment. See
first love's embers long thought dead smolder, years
regress, remembering a puppy love spring
blossoming into summer; mother's fears
abated as my family moved away. Waking.
Carefully, I fold the memories, place
them in my heart, smile having seen your face.

Jon Potter
Rockport, ME

Seeds

We hold inside us
Some packaged seeds, all hard, dry,
Which, shaken, rattle.

When the sun warms earth
We think of planting, set free
The bits held in shells.

So, carefully trench,
Pack soft earth around each seed,
Moisten the garden.

The days flicker past,
Then, like magic, lines of green
Shove aside the earth.

Each green dot reaches
For the sun, for the warm light,
And tickles roots down.

The lift of life, strong,
Pushes toward the blossom now.
Reach for connection.

And when it's reached,
More seeds grow, shelled, protected,
Promising new future.

Yes! Those seeds we hold
Seek the joys of sun and earth.
Open the package.

Jean Marie Martinolich
Bay Saint Louis, MS

A Corded Conversation

My mother used the telephone judiciously. After the operator said, "Number please," she was cordial on the old, black wall-phone but got her business done without wasted words. She looked forward to calling her grown-up children who lived out of town, but in those days, long distance was expensive, so she was counting the minutes throughout the conversation. Eventually, unlimited long distance plans allowed us to stop paying by the minute. Probably, that's why she was always on the other end of the phone line for me, her youngest, never counting minutes or sounding ready to end the conversation and hang up. In the early seventies, Mama traded the old black phone for a yellow wall-phone with a spiral cord that allowed her to stretch almost into the kitchen, enough to keep an eye on something she was cooking. That was the closest she ever came to "multi-tasking" while on a phone conversation. That spiral cord tangled fitfully from being stretched. While my communication range grew wider over the years from updated models, it was from that one pivotal spot, within that slightly extended but limited range allotted to her by the spiral cord, that the remainder of her conversations with me took place. The freedom of a cordless phone allowed me to roam my yard clipping raspberry vines, and beyond, even to check the mailbox across the street, while talking to my mother. With my first cellular, my range expanded even further; I talked to my mother from one state after another, often at the steering wheel, while she stood forever in the same place and was always on the other end of the line for me.

After she died and wasn't anymore, the impulse remained to pick up the phone and call her. I always wanted to tell her about any new interest I suddenly acquired or any of the wacky events that punctuated my daily life, especially after

Jean Marie Martinolich
Bay Saint Louis, MS

moving to the spirited city of New Orleans, where life was ever so colorful. So for a while, I went on talking to her in my head, and responses emerged easily there that felt authentic. She was a good listener—about everyday things, even from the grave. But I rarely discussed deep stuff with her, not even in my own head after she died. On certain topics, her responses were inflexible, simple, and drawn from her religion, from which most of our disagreements surfaced quickly and went nowhere. The subject of religion and many issues surrounding it only served to increase my agitation, especially when she blocked any real discussion with quotes from the catechism. We had a lot of mending to do and our friendly conversation was the healing path towards that.

Before Vatican II, Mama had been a stern Catholic, and her vocabulary in our house for things my much-older sisters did was rife with words that assign degrees of judgment like "mortal" or "venial," or dictatorial like "the infallibility of the Pope," or "Canon Law." Once, she deemed one of my sisters "excommunicated," no longer eligible for the "sacrament." Since those words were used on my sisters, I prepared myself to be impervious to them. I did things that my mother disapproved of, knowing full well there was no "dispensation" forthcoming from Rome for my actions. I could live without the privilege of Papal impunity—a sort of "expungement" some Catholics sought that allows them to divorce and remarry if they claim the right circumstances to get their vow of matrimony "annulled." I overheard these conversations as a child when these avenues were under discussion for two of my sisters, who were both married by the time I was four, and had come home for a stay after an unhappy marriage. I made it plain that neither limbo nor hell would deter me; no priest in the confessional had the power to wipe my sins away. I was unafraid to live a good life despite the risk of whatever the perceived consequences might be. Besides that, I was never going to marry. I dodged any conversation with Mama that I sensed might turn to the "sacred responsibility

Jean Marie Martinolich
Bay Saint Louis, MS

of womanhood." I talked to my father about my rabbits, my horse, and my other pets and their behaviors, but I would not go near those topics with my mother.

Then after Pope John 23rd turned the altars to the people and offered the gentler language of love, not dogma, Mama joined a charismatic prayer group, read Leo Buscaglia, and shifted to expressing Jesus's love. All the time. To everyone. It was such a dramatic shift that I did not trust it. It did not feel authentic. In high school, I put my deeper thoughts into poetry and avoided getting in the car with my mother for any ride more than ten minutes, out of fear that I would not be able to escape the subject. That meant never crossing any bridges in the car with my mother. I got across the Bay on my bicycle and crossed the Lake on the train to get to my first job at the Famous Maker factory in New Orleans, processing orders for men's business suits. I had even avoided discussing my education with her. Thankfully, after my first month on the factory job, my brother asked if I would prefer to go to college. I went through the first year at the university, my decision to drop out, my early married life, the birth of my children, and a divorce from my first husband, steering clear of any serious talk with my mother.

I made it to adulthood without any heavy discussion about sexuality because Mama always tried to tie it into religion or mysticism, and invariably, brought the Virgin Mary into it, even when trying to tell me about menstrual periods. When I was trapped into that lecture, I opened the car window, stretched my head far out to catch a strong breeze from the Gulf that would muffle the sound of her words. Such extreme methods of avoiding challenging talks with her were rarely necessary. Soon I found ways to interest her with topics that distracted us both from the subjects that divided us. All I know is that somehow I grew fond of telling her little stories about something the children did, or about the peculiar ways of the man who sold *The Times Picayune* in front of K & B, about a book by Walker Percy I was reading called *Lost in*

Jean Marie Martinolich
Bay Saint Louis, MS

the Cosmos, or the Saturnalia-Christmas decorations I was making. What started out as an attempt to avoid serious subjects like religion became a quite natural way to talk about an array of other topics, usually springing from something I noticed about my day. These conversations gradually assuaged most wounds. Hard topics, however, remained taboo.

That method of mending worked, almost. Early on, we had one three-month falling-out over the fact that she put religious medals on my first child's diaper pin and took him to be baptized without my permission. I had leverage. I could stop going to see her, as my husband suggested, depriving her of her grandchild. It did not take long. She backed off the pushy behavior she had started ever since the time she called the local priest to come "talk to us" when we moved to Florida.

Despite that, we had begun to enjoy our time together, especially on the phone, even though other rough spots continued. The trouble was more likely to emerge in person. My only time for a visit to see Mama was Sundays. My parents lived in Bay Saint Louis, 59 miles, or one hour away from New Orleans, but she told me not to arrive until her afternoon charismatic prayer group was over. If I arrived early, I grew annoyed listening to what in those days struck me as silly songs. I caught glimpses of the group holding hands and swaying while I sat with my children in the next room waiting. I would seethe, imagining her involved like that as though my time did not matter. Still our friendly but mundane conversations continued, and without even realizing it, I had become dependent on her listening to what was going on at work, in the kitchen, at the grocery store, the gym, or by that time, the classes I had begun. She was a crucial witness to the events of my life. I had no alternative but to accept her charismatic ways. But I remained annoyed, feeling that she was behaving like some sort of Jesus freak. By this time, her knees were turning outward from arthritis and

Jean Marie Martinolich
Bay Saint Louis, MS

her hands were knots; groupies in the broadway musical, *Jesus Christ, Superstar* did not look like my mother. Our phone conversations, however, let us speak a truth that felt authentic, where it was easier to steer clear of religion. She enjoyed my calls, and I needed her to listen. I went on with the stories about everyday life, mostly mine, rarely hers. As though still attached by an umbilical cord, her listening nourished me.

Many years went by and a guarded but sincere relationship developed. I was the child she called from the hospital to stand up for her refusal to accept a feeding tube. She knew that such an intervention would bind her to the hospital indefinitely. My older sisters would not hear her, and my brother, a doctor on staff at that hospital, ignored her request. I was her only post-war, baby-boomer child, her almost back-to-the-earth hippie, the one who had suffered for her sanity against an insane system—she, this woman about to lose her mother at the early age of forty-three, whereas her siblings had nearly twenty more with their mother—she, this baby of the family, was the one Mama asked to set her free to walk out of the hospital against doctor's orders. Together with my mother, I protested the tube feeding and closed the issue. I demonstrated that small spoon feedings, though they took longer, were working. As we left the hospital, the head nurse addressed me, instead of her:

"She can't leave; her lungs are filling with fluid. You can't take her."

With a Gulfport Memorial plastic bag loaded with her belongings, I turned to Mama for verification:

"Did you hear that Mama? Are you aware of what she means?"

"Yes," she confirmed. "I am going home."

So after securing a wheel chair without the help of staff who gathered like militia to tell us she could not leave, we rolled out and headed home.

Jean Marie Martinolich
Bay Saint Louis, MS

I climbed into her bed with her for the last few days of her life. I slept beside her. She made no mention of religion, no mention of the people or priest in her prayer group. I don't know if that was because she no longer wanted to push those topics on me; maybe it was less important to her then, or perhaps it was the many details that crowd the bedside of the dying. Medicines and potty-chairs, how to lift her up in the bed, and the room temperature were natural and authentic topics that left little room for tough conversations—except for one. And it was brief:

"Do you think I have, maybe, another five years?"

"No. I don't. No, Mama, I don't."

After that, we went back to talking like that had never been said. Some sweet words were uttered in the following days, but not much of the serious stuff that some think should be aired between parent and child who have differences. Although I have not used a corded phone in many years, a tiny, barely discernible urge remains to pick up the phone—to hear her lilting voice so ready to listen to me again.

The tough stuff mostly dissipates on its own. What doesn't can wait. It always can.

She was a good listener.

GOOSE RIVER ANTHOLOGY, 2019

We seek selections of fine poetry, essays, and short stories (3,000 words or less) for the 17th annual *Goose River Anthology, 2019.* The book will be beautifully produced with full color cover and full color dust jacket for hard covers.

You may submit even if you have been published before in a previous edition of the *Goose River Anthology.* We retain one-time publishing rights. All rights revert back to the author after publication. You may submit as many pieces as you like.

EARN CASH ROYALTIES. Author will receive a 10% royalty on all sales that he or she generates.

There is no purchase required and nothing is required of the author for publication. Deadline for submissions is April 30, 2019. Publication will be in the fall of 2019 (they make great Christmas gifts). Guidelines are as follows:

- Submit clean, typed copy by snail mail—**mandatory**
- Email a Word or rtf file to us (if possible)
- Reading fee: $1.00 per page
- Do not put two poems on the same page
- Essays and short stories **must be** double-spaced
- **SASE (#10 or larger) for notification** (one forever stamp) plus additional postage for possible return of submission if desired.
- Author's name & address at top of each page of paper copy and first page of emailed copies.

Submit to:
Goose River Anthology, 2019
3400 Friendship Road
Waldoboro, ME 04572-6337
E mail: gooseriverpress@roadrunner.com
www.gooseriverpress.com